Contents

Introduction

What's it like to be a Sikh?

The *Living Faiths* series helps you to learn about religion by meeting some young people and their families in the UK. Through the case studies in this book you will find out first-hand how their faith affects the way they live and the moral and ethical decisions they make. The big question you will explore is: What does it *mean* to be a Sikh in twenty-first century Britain?

The icons indicate where you can actually hear and see young people sharing aspects of their daily lives through film, audio and music. This will help you to reflect on your own experiences, whether you belong to a religion or have a secular view of the world.

Key to icons

 Image gallery
 Audio
 Film
 Worksheet
 Interactive Activity

The Student Book features

Starter activities get you thinking as soon as your lesson starts!

Activities are colour coded to identify three ways of exploring the rich diversity found within and between faiths. Through the questions and activities you will learn to:

- **think like a theologian**: these questions focus on understanding the nature of religious belief, its symbolism and spiritual significance
- **think like a philosopher**: these questions focus on analysing and debating ideas
- **think like a social scientist**: these questions focus on exploring and analysing why people do what they do and how belief affects action

You will be encouraged to think creatively and critically; to empathize, evaluate and respond to the views of others; to give reasons for your opinions and make connections; and draw conclusions.

Useful Words define the key terms which appear in bold, to help you easily understand definitions. Meanings of words are also defined in the glossary.

Reflection

There will be time for you to reflect on what you've learned about the beliefs and practices of others and how they link to your own views.

Assessment

At the end of each chapter there is a final assessment task which helps you to show what you have learned.

Ways of helping you to assess your learning are part of every chapter:

- unit objectives set out what you will learn
- it's easy to see what standards you are aiming for using the 'I can' level statements
- you're encouraged to discuss and assess your own and each other's work
- you will feel confident in recognizing the next steps and how to improve.

We hope that you will enjoy reading and watching young people share their views, and that you will in turn gain the skills and knowledge to understand people with beliefs both similar to and different from your own.

Janet Dyson
(Series Editor)

Robert Bowie
(Series Consultant)

Meet the Families!

In this book, you will meet several young Sikh families from across the UK. You can read about their thoughts and views on various topics covered in the book, and also watch their full interviews on the *Sikhism OxBox Online*.

The Singh/Kaur family

Baltej, Kuljeevan and Dayapreet live in Leicester with their parents, not far from their cousins, Tohmev and Sahib. They are very involved with the local Sikh community and regularly visit their local gurdwara. The boys enjoy playing rugby, cricket and hockey. Baltej and Kuljeevan are also keen fans of Star Wars and any comic cartoon!

Balwir Singh lives with his parents in Southall, and they visit the Southall Gurdwara regularly. Together, the family likes to play sports, and travel to North America and Asia to visit their extended family.

The Singh family

Mejindarpal Kaur

Mejindarpal Kaur is the Legal Director of UNITED SIKHS (www. unitedsikhs.org), an international UN associated advocacy charity which has been in the forefront fighting for human rights and particularly religious rights for Sikhs globally. She led the campaign for the right to wear the turban in France before the UN Human Rights Committee, which held that France had violated the religious rights of Sikhs by banning the turban in schools and on ID photographs.

Overview

Sikhism, known to Sikhs as 'Sikhi', is the youngest of the six main world religions, but has some roots in faith and practices that are much older. The founder of Sikhism is Guru Nanak, who was born into a Hindu family, and wanted nothing more than to worship the One True God, which Sikhs call by many names, including Akal Purakh and Waheguru. He looked beyond the religious practices of the Hindus and Muslims around him at the time and encouraged his followers to search only for God. Sikhism or Sikh means 'student', reminding and focusing the believer on their lifelong journey learning about God.

Sikhism is a faith that is growing and there are more and more communities setting up gurdwaras (Sikh places of worship) around Britain. There are currently around 500,000 Sikhs in the UK with the majority of the world's Sikh population living in the Punjab in India. The total Sikh world population is around 27 million. There are also large Sikh communities in the USA, Canada, Malaysia, East Africa, Australia and Thailand.

The majority of Sikhs are born into the faith, though some do adopt the Sikh way of life. There is no compulsion in Sikhism, which means that a person born as a Sikh will not be shunned if he or she chooses not to practise his or her faith. A growing number of Sikhs have made a commitment to be initiated as the Khalsa, to live a life that is fully focused on God and serving those around them. This commitment also involves wearing certain articles of faith, or Kakaar. This is to help them practise their faith through discipline, and be reminded of the principles of the Khalsa. The ceremony that enables a Sikh to join the Khalsa is called the Amrit Sanskar.

The sacred text Guru Granth Sahib is the eternal guru of the Sikhs. It contains the teachings of the ten Sikh Gurus and also of some Hindu and Muslim holy men, whose beliefs the Gurus shared. The teachings in the Guru Granth Sahib are written in poetic style and in 31 raag or melodic modes. The Guru Granth Sahib begins with the Mool Mantar, a composition of Guru Nanak which contains the essence of Sikh beliefs. Sikhs sing hymns from the Guru Granth Sahib, both during private daily prayer and also during congregational worship at a gurdwara.

Sikhs attend weekly, if not daily, prayers at a gurdwara. This usually happens on a Sunday in the UK, as many people have this day free from work. This is not always a weekly event though, as not all Sikhs have gurdwaras in their local communities, so many worship at home, too. All Sikhs belong to the Sangat or the wider Sikh community, and through participation in the Sangat, feel part of the worldwide family of Sikhs. Sikhs celebrate many festivals throughout the year, including Vaisakhi.

Sikhism is a faith that focuses on a follower's relationship with God and how this is practised each day. There are many beliefs and events that encourage and enable Sikhs in their faith, and there are many ways in which these are expressed. Traditional and modern practices are explored and expressed in this book, as well as how Sikhs face the challenges of living their faith in twenty-first century Britain. To understand more about Sikhism, read on!

1.1 What is at the Root of Sikhism?

Learning Objectives

In this unit you will:

- identify what is at the root of Sikh beliefs
- explain the Mool Mantar and what it shows about Sikh beliefs about God
- reflect on your own mantra for living.

Starter

- 'If God exists, it's obvious that he would be male.'
  Do you agree or disagree with this statement? Why?

Belief in one God is at the root of Sikhism (or Sikhi as it is called by Sikhs). God is viewed as neither male nor female, and is addressed in many different ways by Sikhs. For example, Sikhs sometimes call God 'Akal Purakh', which means 'all-present being that exists throughout the universe'. The term Waheguru or Vaheguru is also used by Sikhs to refer to God or His wonderful teachings.

The opening prayer, or Mool Mantar, in the **Guru Granth Sahib** was written by **Guru Nanak**, the first Sikh **Guru**. The Mool Mantar contains the essence of Sikhism, and describes the attributes of God.

> 'The One who created me takes care of me; He Himself blesses me with glory. […] He is neither a woman, nor a man, nor a bird; the True Lord is so wise and beautiful.'
> Guru Granth Sahib p.1010

Useful Words

Gurdwara The Sikh place of worship

Guru A spiritual teacher

Guru Granth Sahib The eternal guru of the Sikhs, which embodies the teachings of the ten Sikh Gurus

Guru Nanak The founder of Sikhism

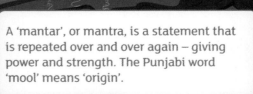

a Just like a seed taking root, a Sikh's source of spirituality is the Mool Mantar.

A 'mantar', or mantra, is a statement that is repeated over and over again – giving power and strength. The Punjabi word 'mool' means 'origin'.

> 'There is One Being who creates, nurtures and destroys; who is the eternal Truth, that exists in its creation, is fearless, without enmity, in timeless form, beyond cycles of rebirth, was self-created, and may be attained with Grace.'
> The Mool Mantar (Guru Granth Sahib p.1)

Case Study

Mr Singh and Mrs Kaur live in Leicester with their children Baltej, Kuljeevan and Dayapreet. They are practising Sikhs who regularly worship God at home and in the **gurdwara**. For them, the Mool Mantar is more than just words – it plays a daily part in their lives:

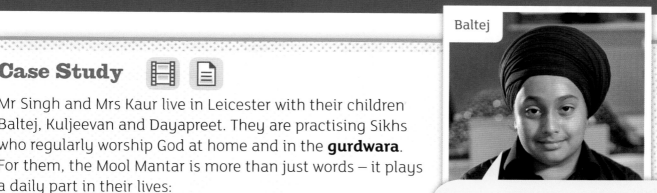

Baltej

It's important in my life, because it reminds me about God. When I think about God, it reminds me that our actions should be good and that we should respect people equally.

I think the Mool Mantar is significant for everybody – the message is universal. It's the definition of God. You can go into different situations and you can think: "God is not being fair", but God is doing what is right for you. Remembering that whatever He does is truth can help us. You can have a disagreement with individuals, and know that God doesn't discriminate, is fearless and loves everybody. It's reassuring – and it's good to know that He's not going to look at you differently.

Mr Singh

For Sikhs, it's an easy prayer to start off the day, because it's simple. It's not long, the meanings are very simple and it's simple to repeat the words. There is not a lot to learn, so it can be understood and used from a young age.

Mrs Kaur

Reflection

Create your own (non-religious) mantra. Do you think that repeating it could strengthen and empower you?

Activities

1. The Mool Mantar expresses beliefs that are at the root of the Sikh faith. Why do you think Sikhs say it at least once a day? Use the case study information to show how it makes a difference to the daily lives of the Singh/Kaur family.

2. Which of the descriptions of God from the Mool Mantar do you think is the most difficult to understand? Share your thoughts with a partner and work together to see if you can explain the words and ideas you find difficult.

3. Design a piece of artwork, using the symbolism of the root as a border for the words of the Mool Mantar. Remember that the word 'mool' means 'origin', and think about the idea that Sikh spirituality grows and draws sustenance from the Mool Mantar.

4. Sikhs believe that life is about putting God at the root of life – rather than human, materialistic desires. How do you think the Mool Mantar helps them to achieve this?

Learning Objectives

In this unit you will:

- examine Sikh beliefs about the characteristics of God
- explain the meaning and significance of Waheguru
- reflect on the symbolism of darkness and light.

Starter

- Discuss with a partner: 'Are you, or have you ever been, afraid of the dark? Why do you think many people fear darkness?'

The opening phrase of the Mool Mantar, 'ik oankar', can be briefly translated as 'There is One Being who creates, nurtures and destroys'. Sikhs have many names to describe the one god – each with a special significance. For example, Waheguru (pronounced Va-hi-goo-roo) means 'Wondrous Enlightener', or 'Wonderful Lord'. By breaking down the word into its component parts, we can see where this description comes from. Simply put, 'wahe' means 'wondrous' or 'inspiring', 'gu' means 'darkness' and 'ru' means 'light'. Therefore, Sikhs believe that, in a spiritual sense, Waheguru is one who removes darkness and brings light.

b The letters in Gurmukhi that make up the Ik Oankar are often used by Sikhs as a religious sign in homes or on objects of adoration.

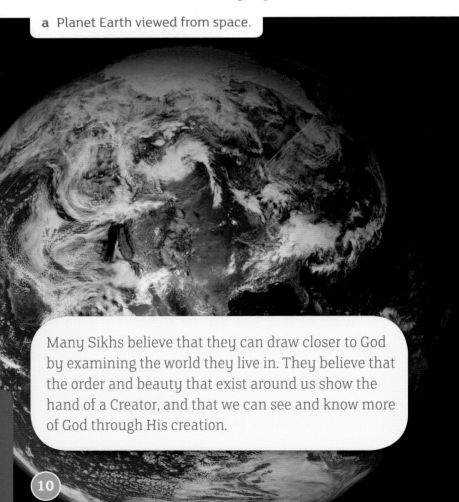

a Planet Earth viewed from space.

Many Sikhs believe that they can draw closer to God by examining the world they live in. They believe that the order and beauty that exist around us show the hand of a Creator, and that we can see and know more of God through His creation.

? Find or create images, and choose words about light and dark, to create a symbol or collage showing the Sikh belief that Waheguru brings spiritual light.

'If a hundred moons were to rise, and a thousand suns appeared, even with such light, there would still be pitch darkness without the Guru.'
Guru Granth Sahib p.463

Guru Nanak taught that constant spiritual practice should be part of a Sikh's daily life. A Sikh will therefore do Nit Naem prayers – daily prayers in the morning, evening and at bed time. As well as this, a Sikh focuses on the name of God through Simran or **meditation**, at any or all times of the day. Simran involves the repeated chanting of Waheguru Mantar or parts of the Mool Mantar. Sikhs believe 'remembering' God in this way brings them closer to Him.

Reflection

What do you see as the darkness and light in life?

c Sikh worshippers singing 'Waheguru' in a London gurdwara.

Activities

1. Explain, in your own words, how Sikhs believe that the world around them shows something of God's nature.

2. Look at a newspaper or watch a news broadcast. What stories might be difficult to see as fitting with the Sikh view of seeing God in nature? Explain your thinking. How might a Sikh respond, based on what you know?

3. Some of the Sikh beliefs about God can be summed up with the following phrase: 'Just as fragrance is in the flower, and reflection is in the mirror, in just the same way, God is within you.' Explain what you think this means.

4. What questions do you think Sikhs ask about God? What would you like to ask about the God that Sikhism describes?

5. In what ways does light and dark help to understand the idea of a divine being?

1.3 Soldiers and Saints: The Symbolism of the Khanda

Learning Objectives

In this unit you will:

- explain the origins and significance of the **Khanda** symbol
- apply some key points of the **Reht Maryada**
- reflect on the role of duty in your own life.

Starter

- What duties are you required to fulfil in your life (at home, school, work, with friends)?

The Khanda is a Sikh symbol that reveals what is important to a Sikh – and what they stand for. The symbol contains three swords and a circle, with different meanings as explained below.

The right-hand sword (Piri) represents spirituality.

The left-hand sword (Miri) reminds Sikhs of their willingness to fight for what is right in the world.

The double-edged sword in the middle (also called a Khanda) unites the other two swords together and reminds Sikhs that there is one God.

The circle around the middle (the Chakkar) represents the eternal love and nature of God.

a The Khanda symbol is often worn as a turban pin or embroidered on ceremonial clothing.

Case Study

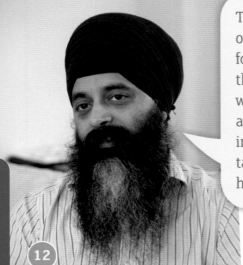

The Khanda is our emblem. It reminds us of being both a soldier and a saint, who follows God's word. The key thing is that the saintly aspect comes first; a soldier without spiritual grounding could make a wrong decision that might kill or harm innocent people. The Sikh scriptures first taught us to be a saint, but you have to have the conviction to help others as well.

Tohmev is a cousin in the Singh/Kaur family. He says: 'I learned about the Khanda from my parents. We used to put it on our Dastaars [turbans]. You have to be a saint, helping the needy, and a soldier, which is more about protecting the needy and fighting for justice.'

The Khanda is not the only thing that can guide a Sikh in their actions. There is also, amongst other things, the Sikh Reht Maryada. This is the Sikh code of conduct – including how to live life as an individual and as part of the Sikh community, how services should be run in a gurdwara, and the significance of the teachings of the Gurus.

The Reht Maryada upholds the three main duties that Sikhs have to complete in life – which are both spiritual and earthly goals (see the diagram). The three duties are very simple but very significant – as a minimum, a Sikh should perform these three duties daily.

? Why do you think the three duties are some of the most important things for a Sikh to do? They could be shortened into three words: pray, work, give. What three words could you use to describe your duties in life?

Nam japo: Keep God in mind at all times

b The three main Sikh duties.

Kirt kero: Earn an honest living (since God is truth, a Sikh should live honestly)

Vand chhako: Give to charity and care for others (see Unit 3.6)

Reflection
What would life be like if you had no duties or obligations?

Activities

1 Explain in three sentences how the Khanda might help a Sikh in the modern world.

2 Look carefully at the three duties from the Reht Maryada in the above diagram. Some people believe that duty should be completed without worrying about whether you get any reward for it. Do you think a Sikh would agree with this? What is your own opinion?

3 Can you be both a saint and a soldier? Can you be a soldier without being violent or harming anyone? Design a business card for each role, giving your answer through what you include on the card.

4 Identify the symbolism of the Khanda, and then create a logo for yourself that is made up of three objects that are significant to you.

1.4 After Death, After Life – What Lives On?

Learning Objectives

In this unit you will:

- explain Sikh beliefs about life and death
- evaluate why Sikhs believe that the human life is precious for seeking and obtaining union with God
- reflect on whether you should live for more than the moment.

Starter

- Do you think that there is a part of a person that will never die?

Sikhism teaches that all humans have a **soul** (**atma**) – a divine spark which is the most important part of a human being. The soul does not die, it is **reincarnated** into the next life. Physical death is a means by which the soul travels from one form to another until it achieves union with God.

Sikhs believe that they will reap what they sow – how they live their life has a direct impact on their spiritual growth in this life and the next. Everything they think, say and do is recorded – and produces either good or bad **karma**. This karma dictates what type of life they will be reborn into.

Those who live a **gurmukh**-focused (God-centred) life, rather than a **manmukh**-focused (materialistic) life, will be much more likely to ensure positive karma – and so a positive cycle of reincarnation. This is why the three duties (see Unit 1.3) are so important. The ultimate goal is to break free from the cycle of reincarnation by gaining **mukti** for the soul. The way to do this is to earn only positive karma.

Useful Words

Gurmukh Putting God at the centre of your life

Karma A combination of a person's actions, with either a positive or negative outcome in the next life

Manmukh Putting human and materialistic desires at the centre of your life

Mukti Union of the soul with God

Reincarnation A cycle of birth and death and rebirth

Soul (atma) The spiritual spark that keeps the body alive

? Sikhs believe that the human form is precious, as in this form they can seek mukti through their actions. They may be reincarnated into any form (human, plant, animal, etc.) to allow the soul to travel until it obtains union with God. What do you think about this idea? How would you change this diagram to make it show what you believe?

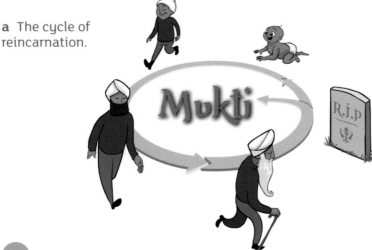

a The cycle of reincarnation.

Case Study

Balwir Singh is a Sikh who worships at the gurdwara in Southall, London. He believes in reincarnation and the concept of karma.

Balwir explains a little more about how his actions are recorded and added to his karma by telling the Sikh story of two angels, Chitar and Gupat, who sit on each of his shoulders noting down all his deeds.

The angels write down if I have prayed or if I haven't; if I have done anything bad, or if I swore at someone. They write it all down.

Although Balwir doesn't believe this story literally, he uses it as a good illustration of karma:

When a Sikh dies, the story goes that the two angels will travel with the soul to Dharm-Raj (the righteous judge put in place by God to decide whether the soul gets reincarnated or not). If the soul has more negative than positive karma, it might get reincarnated as a lower life form (or into a human life that's not as good as the previous one). If the soul's karma is completely positive, then it will gain mukti.

Balwir also talks about the Five Vices in Sikhism that bring about negative karma: lust, greed, attachment to things of this world, anger, and pride. A Sikh will aim to remove these vices from their lives.

? What kinds of behaviour could contribute towards bad karma? Think about your own life – do you think that you could be described as having positive or negative karma at the moment?

Reflection

'Live life for the moment. Worry about the rest another time.' Do you agree with this view? Why or why not?

Activities

1. Prepare a short paragraph to teach a Year 5 class about the Sikh beliefs on life and death. Make sure that you include all the Useful Words.

2. Is Balwir's story about the angels simply a story for children, or could it have a deeper meaning about good and bad actions? Explain your ideas to a partner.

3. An atheist (someone who doesn't believe in God) would argue that there is no life after death at all. Does this mean they don't have to worry about how they behave?

4. How might someone who believes in karma live their life differently from someone who doesn't?

5. Discuss the 'Five Vices' in small groups. What are they? In what ways are they significant?

6. What's wrong with pride or attachment to things of this world? Consider two responses to this question.

What do Sikhs Believe?

Objectives

- Explore and apply the key beliefs that Sikhs have about God and duty.
- Reflect on your own ideas about God and the responsibilities you have in your life.

Task

Prepare a presentation or a leaflet to be used as a resource in RE, in answer to the question: Who is a Sikh? You will need to explain what Sikhs believe about God, including the significance of the Mool Mantar. The final part of your presentation or leaflet should contain your own reflections about core Sikh beliefs.

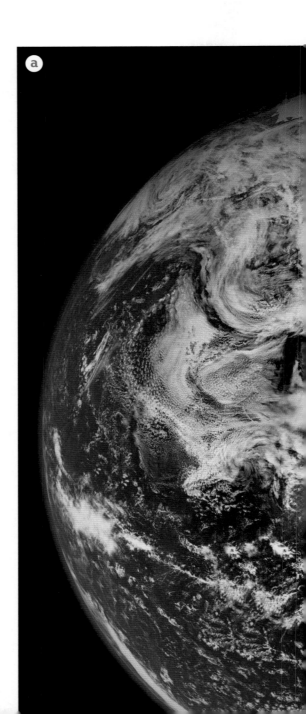

a

A bit of guidance...

You should aim to summarize the core Sikh beliefs, and then consider what impact they might have on a Sikh's life. Think carefully about the words that Sikhs use to describe God, the core duties they perform, and how their actions in this life might affect their life after death.

Hints and tips

To help you tackle this task, you could:

- read through this chapter, noting down the key Sikh beliefs and using them to structure your leaflet or presentation
- conduct some independent research to improve your work with interesting up-to-date stories or examples
- try to include interesting facts or illustrations that would appeal to an audience of students your own age.

Guidance

What level are you aiming at? Have a look at the grid below to see what you need to do to achieve that level. What would you need to do to improve your work?

	I can...
Level 3	• use religious vocabulary to describe some key features of Sikh beliefs about God • ask important questions about Sikhism and Sikh beliefs about God – making links between my own responses and those of others.
Level 4	• use a range of religious vocabulary to describe and show understanding of the sources and beliefs held by Sikhs about God • raise and suggest answers to questions about belonging, meaning, truth and commitment to a Sikh belief in God.
Level 5	• use a wide range of religious vocabulary to explain the impact of a Sikh belief in God on individuals and communities • ask and suggest answers to questions about belonging, meaning, truth and commitment to a Sikh belief in God – relating them to my own life and those of others.
Level 6	• use religious and philosophical language to give detailed accounts of Sikh belief, and others' disbelief, in God – explaining any reasons for the differences between them • use argument and examples to show the links between beliefs, teachings and experiences from a range of people.

Ready for more?

When you have completed this task, you can also work on your skills for Levels 6 and 7, and perhaps even higher. This is an extension task.

'My identity isn't just about who I am, it's about what I believe. My beliefs make me who I am.'

Do you agree or disagree? Why is having a sense of identity important?

2.1 Guru Nanak Sahib Ji

Learning Objectives

In this unit you will:

- explain the relevance of Guru Nanak's upbringing and teaching
- analyse the nature of a **religious experience**
- reflect on your own life-changing experiences.

Guru Nanak founded Sikhism and, therefore, is highly respected by all Sikhs. He is often given the title of 'Guru Nanak Sahib Ji' (the additional words 'Sahib Ji' mean that he is a respected Master). He wrote many of the teachings in the Guru Granth Sahib.

Guru Nanak was born into a Hindu family in 1469 – in an area where there was a lot of fighting between Hindus and Muslims. As he grew up, he showed great interest in religious belief and studied Hinduism and Islam extensively.

As he was born into a Hindu family, Guru Nanak was due to start wearing the Hindu **sacred thread** at the age of 13, but he refused – saying that the internal changes that people make to adopt good qualities are far more significant than any external things they might wear. He continued to make this point – arguing with religious leaders that external elements, such as pilgrimages, are less important than internal changes to an individual's soul and their relationship with God.

Useful Words

Religious experience An experience of God; a spiritual experience

Sacred thread A cord worn as a Hindu rite of passage

? Guru Nanak taught that the internal soul, and its connection with God, is more important than external actions. Bearing this in mind, what can you say about Guru Nanak from this picture? What do you think the artist is trying to show?

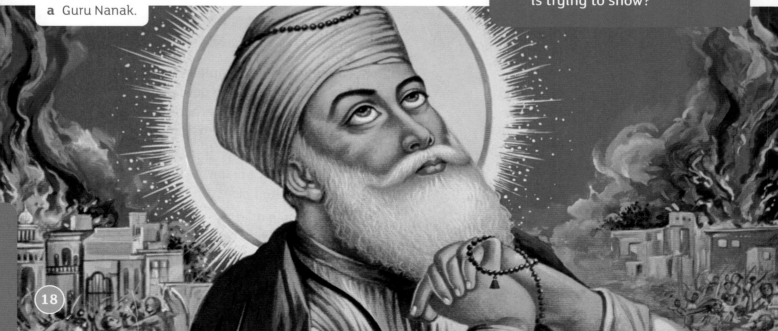

a Guru Nanak.

Guru Nanak and the River

One day, when he was 30 years old, Guru Nanak went down to the river with his friend to bathe. Suddenly, to his friend's horror, Guru Nanak disappeared under the water. Even though the river was dragged, and many people searched for him, he could not be found. Therefore, he was presumed dead. However, after three days – to everyone's amazement – Guru Nanak simply walked out of the river, unharmed.

Guru Nanak did not speak for days afterwards. Then he said: 'There is no Muslim, there is no Hindu'. He went on to explain that when he was in the river, he had the powerful feeling that he was being swept into God's presence. His experience of God made him realize that the external, religious elements that people fight over were trivial – and that religious labels were not important. The only important thing was following the way of the One God. Guru Nanak then spent his time travelling and teaching that true spirituality goes beyond all religions.

b Guru Nanak emerges from the river.

? Do you think it's possible to have an experience of a divine being? Do you think that anyone can experience God, or just a chosen few? Give reasons for your answers.

'The Hindu worships at the temple, the Muslim at the mosque. Naam Dayv (a Sikh saint) serves that Lord who is not limited to either the temple or the mosque. […] One Universal Creator God.'
Guru Granth Sahib p.875

Reflection

Have you ever had a life-changing experience? How did it affect you?

Activities

1. Explore the deeper meanings of the story above about Guru Nanak's spiritual experience. Read the story carefully and think of two questions that you would like to explore with a partner or group.

2. Put Guru Nanak's friend in the 'Hot Seat'. Prepare questions to examine how he felt about Guru Nanak's spiritual experience.

3. Guru Nanak believed religious labels are not important. Why might some people find this idea troubling? What is gained by a strong sense of a common identity?

4. Think about the meaning of the above quotation from the Guru Granth Sahib. Use it to help explain why you think Guru Nanak said: 'There is no Muslim, there is no Hindu.'

5. What would be lost and what might be gained in a world where all religions agreed?

Learning Objectives

In this unit you will:

- identify some of Guru Nanak's key teachings
- explain the role of Guru Nanak's teachings in a Sikh's life
- reflect on the qualities of a good teacher.

Starter

- How and when do you learn best? Note down your thoughts.

As the founder of Sikhism, Guru Nanak is held in the highest regard by Sikhs. They believe that he was one of the wisest and holiest men in Sikh history. He taught many things during his lifetime, and his teachings can be found in the Guru Granth Sahib. One of the stories relating to Guru Nanak's teachings on honest living is illustrated below.

? What do you think the story of Malik Bhago is teaching? Is it still relevant in the twenty-first century?

Malik Bhago and Bhai Lalo

This story is about two men – the dishonest and corrupt Malik Bhago, and a poor but loving man called Bhai Lalo. Guru Nanak was offered impressive, rich food by Malik Bhago. He was also offered simple, honest food by Bhai Lalo. Guru Nanak took the rich food, squeezed it and blood dripped out. Then he took the simple food, squeezed it and milk flowed out.

a Guru Nanak squeezes the food offerings from the two men.

Case Study

Mr Singh values all the Gurus' teachings, but what stands out for him the most are the three duties, taught by Guru Nanak (see Unit 1.3):

I think it's important to make a truthful, honest, earnest living, so the work you do is honest and you have a daily job to earn money so that you can give money to charity and feed your family [...] The second duty is to share with others, and the third is to contemplate on God – to tune your mind back into God. These three are basic teachings but are very important, because working honestly and sharing and meditating are three great things for us to do and live by.

? Think of somebody you admire. What single principle or belief would you take from their life and apply to yours? Why?

Activities

❶ Consider the story opposite. What is the moral of the story? What links can you make between the story and the three duties mentioned in the case study?

❷ What values are expressed in the photo of Mr Singh on this page? Think about objects, dress, expression, and stance.

❸ Read through the comments from Mr Singh in the case study. What would you ask him if you could?

❹ 'Without wisdom, you cannot teach. Unless you teach, you cannot lead.' How would you respond to this statement?

❺ What are the top three qualities of a teacher? Do you think a guru should have these qualities?

Reflection

After completing Activity 4 below, revisit your response to the starter question. Do the qualities that you identify in a good teacher affect the ways in which you learn?

2.3 The Tremendous Ten (Part A)

Learning Objectives

In this unit you will:

- explain the role and significance of the ten Sikh Gurus
- explain the impacts of the lives and actions of the Gurus
- explore to what extent a role model can 'lead'.

Starter

- Think of as many superheroes as you can. What, apart from their powers, made them super?
- If you could be a superhero, what would your superpower be?

The ten Sikh Gurus were an incredible group of people. They lived during the period from the fifteenth to the eighteenth centuries, beginning with Guru Nanak (the founding Guru), who was born in 1469. The remaining nine Gurus taught, one after the other – providing a source of teaching and experience that built up over 200 years. Even though the teachings of all the Gurus were the same, each Guru is known for something different about the Sikh faith. Now find out more about the Tremendous Ten …

Sikhs do not worship images of the Gurus, as it is the teachings and example of the Gurus that they respect and value. These images are an artist's impression.

Guru Angad (1504–1552): the right to education for all

Guru Angad, who was then called Bhai Lehna, devoted seven years to living under the guidance of Guru Nanak. After many tests, Guru Nanak appointed Bhai Lehna as his successor and the second Sikh Guru in 1539.

Guru Angad focused on the work that Guru Nanak had already started, but he also added some very significant elements of his own. He valued education and the right of all – children and adults – to learn.

Guru Nanak (1469–1539): the founder of the Sikh faith

Guru Nanak inspired many through his example and his teachings (See Units 2.1 and 2.2).

Useful Words

Castes Groups and/or divisions within society with higher or lower status than each other
Creeds Statements of belief, usually religious
Pilgrimage A holy journey to a place of religious significance

? Guru Nanak knew his successor had to be worthy of the title. Guru Angad was a devoted follower of Guru Nanak's teachings and example, but would he make a good leader? It is believed that Guru Nanak put Guru Angad through a series of tests. What do you think they were, and what do you think Guru Nanak was looking for?

Guru Amar Das (1479–1574): the establishment of the Langar

Guru Amar Das:

- was appointed Guru Angad's successor and the third Sikh Guru, because he proved himself worthy and devoted
- is particularly remembered for fully committing the Sikh faith to the Langar (the free kitchen open to all)
- made sure that Emperors, Rajas and anyone of a higher status in society sat and ate together at the same level as those of the lowest status.

(For more about the Langar, see Unit 3.6.)

Guru Ram Das (1534–1581): the founder of the Golden Temple

Guru Ram Das:

- was appointed by Guru Amar Das as his successor – being his most worthy and humble follower
- established the Sikh wedding ceremony (see Unit 3.4)
- founded the Sikh holy city of Amritsar in the Punjab region of India. At the heart of the city is the Gurdwara Harmandir Sahib – translated as the 'abode of God'. It is also known as the Golden Temple. This is now a place of great holiness for Sikhs and many go on **pilgrimage** to see it.

Guru Arjan (1563–1606): respect for everyone

Guru Arjan:

- was the youngest son of Guru Ram Das, who succeeded his father as the fifth Sikh Guru and continued his father's work in Amritsar
- said 'My faith is for the people of all **castes** and all **creeds** from whichever direction they come and to whichever direction they bow'
- collected the writings of all five Gurus up to this point into the Adi Granth, or Guru Granth Sahib
- respected people of all faiths and included the writings of Hindu and Muslim scholars that reflected the teachings of Sikhism

? Religious intolerance is not new. Explain to a partner why you think people fight about religion. Some people argue that it's more about power or politics than religion. Discuss this point.

Reflection

What do you think is the most important theme in life: education, equality, love, or respect? Create a Haiku (or short poem that does not rhyme) explaining your choice.

Guru Har Gobind (1595–1644): equality and justice for all

Guru Har Gobind was the son of Guru Arjan. When he was appointed as the sixth Sikh Guru, he asked for two swords — saying that one sword would represent his authority on Earth, and the other would show his spiritual authority. These two swords are represented in the Khanda (see Unit 1.3). Guru Har Gobind prepared the Sikhs for both spiritual and earthly battles, and encouraged equal treatment for all.

? Reflect on the two swords of authority that Guru Har Gobind took. If you were to lead the people around you, would you rather focus your leadership campaign on practical 'earthly' issues, or moral and 'spiritual' issues? Design a campaign poster which explains your choice.

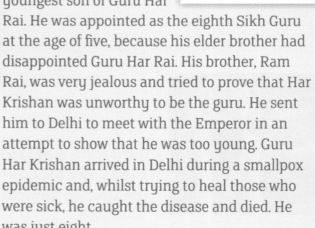

Guru Har Krishan (1656–1664): the five-year-old Guru

Guru Har Krishan was the youngest son of Guru Har Rai. He was appointed as the eighth Sikh Guru at the age of five, because his elder brother had disappointed Guru Har Rai. His brother, Ram Rai, was very jealous and tried to prove that Har Krishan was unworthy to be the guru. He sent him to Delhi to meet with the Emperor in an attempt to show that he was too young. Guru Har Krishan arrived in Delhi during a smallpox epidemic and, whilst trying to heal those who were sick, he caught the disease and died. He was just eight.

Guru Har Rai (1630–1661): man of peace

Guru Har Rai was the grandson of Guru Har Gobind. He had impressed his grandfather with his sensitivity to all living things. Although he maintained the military developments of his grandfather, Guru Har Rai was a man of peace who discouraged the slaughter of animals in hunting (preferring to keep them alive in his zoo). He also maintained good relations with the ruling Muslim leaders — and once helped to save the life of the Emperor with a herbal remedy he had made.

? Which modern-day Sikh beliefs are reflected in Guru Har Rai's life?

? Should there be more children in positions of authority these days? What do you think would happen if all the leaders at your school were replaced with children — what could they bring to the role?

Guru Tegh Bahadur (1621–1675): challenging religious persecution

The Sikhs had been told by Guru Har Krishan to look for their next guru in the village of Bakala, but a number of Sikhs claimed to be the guru. Guru Tegh Bahadur (the youngest son of the sixth Guru, Guru Har Gobind) was found in meditation in the village. He had learned a lot since he left his father to spend time studying the scriptures, and he was ready to assume the role of guru. He is especially remembered for his response to the Emperor Aurengzeb, who was forcing conversions to Islam through tyranny. Hindus, in particular, were being persecuted. Guru Tegh Bahadur met with the Emperor to defend the Hindus' right to practise their own faith. He ended up being tortured, as well as having to watch his friends and fellow Sikhs being brutally killed. Then, he was publicly beheaded – sacrificing himself to save the freedom of another religion.

Guru Gobind Singh (1666-1708): final human Guru and founder of the Khalsa

Guru Gobind Singh was the tenth Sikh Guru. He felt that his role was to maintain justice and fight oppression of the weak. He made some of the greatest changes to the Sikh faith – not only by establishing the Khalsa (see Units 2.6, 3.1 and 3.2), but also by declaring that there would be no more human Gurus. The Guru Granth Sahib (see Unit 2.5) was named as Guru Gobind Singh's successor, and Sikhs treat it with great respect and significance.

Reflection

What advice would you give to someone who was about to take on a responsible leadership role?

Activities

1. Create your own fact file for someone you consider to be a role model, and then compare it with one of the fact files for the ten Sikh Gurus.

2. Explain, in one sentence, what you think links all ten Sikh Gurus together.

3. In pairs, write a magazine interview with two of the Sikh Gurus. Ask them to explain their lives, focusing on what they love and what they are committed to.

4. Sikhs believe that the Gurus can bring light into their lives through their example and teachings. If someone saw you as a role model, what would you like it to be for?

5. In a group, describe how you would create an advertisement to make people want to go and hear one of the Sikh Gurus speak, were they alive today.

Learning Objectives

In this unit you will:

- identify the relationship between the ten human Gurus and the Guru Granth Sahib
- examine the significance of the Guru Granth Sahib for Sikhs
- reflect on the topic of respect.

Starters

- Do you have a book, a piece of writing, or some song lyrics, that are special to you? Why are they special?

Although the eternal Guru (the Guru Granth Sahib) is not a human being, Sikhs treat it with the same respect that they would show if it were a human guru. As you learned in Units 2.3 and 2.4, the Guru Granth Sahib is the Sikh holy book – a guide for life made up of the teachings and writings of Sikh Gurus. It is, therefore, very precious within Sikhism. Balwir Singh explains the importance of the Guru Granth Sahib.

Sikhs do not worship the Guru Granth Sahib, but they show their respect for it in a number of ways. These include not turning their backs on it, removing their shoes and covering their heads in its presence. Also, no one can ever sit at a higher level than the Guru Granth Sahib.

When the Guru Granth Sahib was first put together by Guru Arjan (the fifth Guru), he included holy writings from Hindus and Muslims. This is because the Gurus recognized that God's universal truths are not limited to one person or faith. Sikhs believe that there is only one God and that His words can be found in other faiths, too.

Case Study

The ritual of human gurus has stopped now, so there will be no other guru from now on – only the Guru Granth Sahib. We have been told that if we have any questions, we should read the Guru Granth Sahib and we will get an answer, no matter what it is.

a Crowds gather at a gurdwara to hear from the Guru Granth Sahib.

Case Study

Some people might ask why the Guru Granth Sahib is made up of the writings of all the Gurus – and not just Guru Nanak, the founding Guru. Balwir Singh explains why.

From the first to the tenth, all Gurus taught so many people – giving them knowledge about how to live, and finally ending with the completion of the Guru Granth Sahib. The Gurus prepared the religion of Sikhism. It doesn't take one brick to make a building – it takes a lot of time and effort. That is why the ten Gurus all helped to make the whole building, and now the Guru Granth Sahib is here.

All teachings are equal, but one that stands out is about the nature of God. God has many names like Allah, Ram, Waheguru, but they are all God's name. There is only one God, and it doesn't matter if you are good, or bad, or what faith you belong to – we are all the same. We are like rivers going to the same ocean in the end.

Many Sikhs read the Guru Granth Sahib every day. Balwir reads it often via the Internet, because keeping such a holy book at home can be difficult. To the right, he talks about the teachings that are special to him.

b

? Why might it be difficult for Sikhs to keep their holy book at home?

Activities

1. What benefits is Balwir Singh getting from reading the Guru Granth Sahib regularly?

2. **a** If you could combine together the writings or sayings of a number of people, who would they be? Why?

   b What image or symbol would you have on your front cover? Explain your choice and what you hope people would get from it.

Reflection

Is there enough respect in the world today? What or who do you show respect to?

3. 'A book can hold a thousand ideas and all the answers we need for any time and any place.' How would you respond to this statement? How does it link to the Guru Granth Sahib?

Learning Objectives

In this unit you will:

- explain the origins of the Khalsa
- interpret the meaning of faith
- reflect on personal commitment and what it involves.

The story of how the Khalsa began is a dramatic and heroic one. It happened in 1699 at the celebration of the spring festival of Vaisakhi.

The Story of the Khalsa

Guru Gobind Singh ordered the Sikhs to meet together in Anandapur. To the astonishment of the crowd, the Guru came out of his tent, and demanded the head of a loyal Sikh as a sign of ultimate commitment. One man came forward and went into the tent. The sound of a blow was heard and the Guru emerged, a bloodied sword in his hand. The crowd was horrified as the Guru asked for more men to come forward. Another man offered his life. This happened again and again until five men had offered their lives to the Guru.

Suddenly, to the amazement of the crowd, the Guru appeared with the five men. They were unhurt, and were dressed in saffron robes and turbans, with blue sashes. Guru Gobind Singh honoured the men with the title Panj Piare, or the Five Beloved Ones. He then initiated them as the first members of the Khalsa, and also sought initiation into the Khalsa himself. The initiation involved taking Amrit (a sweet mixture of sugar and water). Many others that day chose to follow the example of the five brave Sikhs.

a Guru Gobind Singh appears with the Five Beloved Ones.

The formation of the Khalsa is celebrated with great joy each year during the festival of Vaisakhi (see Unit 3.5). It reminds Sikhs of the importance of their commitment to their faith and the fact that they are part of a wider community.

The Khalsa is still growing today. It is the community of Sikhs who have decided to show a further commitment to their faith by being initiated as one of the 'beloved' or, as the word Khalsa means, 'pure'. Not every Sikh chooses to do this but most do, and this further demonstration of their faith is expressed physically through both the Amrit ceremony and the daily wearing of five key items known as the Five Ks (see Unit 3.2).

The Amrit ceremony takes place in the gurdwara in the presence of the Guru Granth Sahib. Those who take part must be prepared to accept the rules and responsibilities of belonging to the Sikh community, and promise to keep the vows. After prayers have been said, each person drinks Amrit, which is then sprinkled on their eyes and heads. They are now initiated members of the Sangat, or Sikh community, and must keep the Five Ks.

b A Sikh takes part in the Amrit ceremony, in a gurdwara in Birmingham.

Reflection

What makes you put your trust in someone?

Activities

1 Finish this sentence: 'The original Panj Piare showed their faith by …'

2 Reread, or listen to, the story about the formation of the Khalsa. Work in pairs to explore questions raised by the story. For example: Was it acceptable for the Guru to deceive the Sikhs in order to win their loyalty? What inspires faith? Is faith the same as trust?

3 Imagine that you were in the crowd listening to Guru Gobind Singh and watching the events as they happened. How do you think you would have reacted? Write a series of texts as if you were there, recording your reactions.

4 Imagine that you are Guru Gobind Singh before the festival of Vaisakhi, knowing what you are going to do. Write a letter to those who you believe will offer their lives, explaining why you are going to ask for their sacrifice and why they are so special for volunteering.

5 'Trust is the most important value of all.' Discuss this idea and consider two possible responses.

Where do Sikh Beliefs Come From?

Objectives

- Examine the key people, places and events that contributed to the beliefs and practices of Sikhism, and present them in ways that enable others to understand their significance.

- Identify and re-tell stories that are important to Sikhs.

Task

Use the information about the key people, places and events in Sikhism in Chapter 2 to create *A Little Book of Sikh Stories* suitable for use in RE lessons for children aged eight or nine. Illustrate your cover and the stories in the book.

a

A bit of guidance...

- Look back at the stories about the ten Sikh Gurus in this chapter. Consider the different contributions that each one made – bearing in mind that every Guru is very significant in Sikhism.

- You will need to look at the themes that are central to Sikhism, and then look at who contributed the most to these themes.

- Select the information that you think is most important and most interesting.

Hints and tips

- Make sure that you identify the key points and ideas in each of the stories you have chosen to tell

- Use language that is appropriate for children aged eight or nine

- Keep your stories interesting

- Don't make them too long

- Show how each story relates to Sikh beliefs

- Try reading your stories out loud to a partner to see how well they work

Guidance

What level are you aiming at? Have a look at the grid below to see what you need to do to achieve that level. What would you need to do to improve your work?

	I can...
Level 3	• use a developing religious vocabulary to describe some key stories in Sikhism • ask important questions about Sikhism and Sikh beliefs, making links between my own and others' responses.
Level 4	• use a developing religious vocabulary to describe and show understanding of Sikh stories, practices, beliefs and ideas • raise and suggest answers to questions of identity, meaning, belonging, purpose and truth.
Level 5	• use an increasingly wide religious vocabulary to explain how stories impact the beliefs of individuals and the wider Sikh community • ask and suggest answers to questions of identity, meaning, belonging, purpose and truth – relating them to my own and others' lives.
Level 6	• use religious and philosophical vocabulary to give an informed account of Sikhism and its beliefs, via key stories • use reasoning and examples to express insights into the relationship between beliefs and teachings, plus questions of identity, belonging, meaning and truth.

Ready for more?

When you have completed this task, you can also work on your skills for Levels 6 and 7, and perhaps even higher. This is an extension task.

'Religious beliefs are more influenced by the time in which they are established, or the culture in which they are founded.' Do you agree or disagree? Use stories from Sikhism to inform your answer.

To achieve the higher levels, you will need to look at the influence of history and culture on aspects of Sikh belief, as well as asking and answering questions about identity, belonging, meaning and truth.

3.1 Belonging to the Khalsa

Learning Objectives

In this unit you will:

- explain what it means to belong to the Khalsa
- identify and explain the significance of the Five Ks
- reflect on your own experiences of belonging.

Starter

- How many places have you lived in your life? Where do you feel you belong? What makes you feel you belong? How do you show that you belong?

The Khalsa is the community of initiated Sikhs who want to make a higher level of commitment to their faith. What does it mean to belong to the Khalsa for Sikhs in Britain today?

? Before looking at Unit 3.2, which gives more detail about the meaning and symbolism of the Five Ks, think back over what you have already learned and suggest what you think the meaning might be.

Case Study

Balwir Singh is a committed member of the Khalsa. For Balwir, the Khalsa is much more than the wider, initiated Sikh community.

The purpose of the Khalsa is to respect the poor, defend the weak, and understand that everyone is equal. Members of the Khalsa often see themselves as spiritual warriors, battling for the rights of those in need.

Sikhs demonstrate their membership of the Khalsa by committing to perform daily prayer (the Nit Naem), and also by wearing the Five Ks (see Unit 3.2). Balwir explains a little more below.

The Five Ks are the Kesh (which is uncut hair), Kangha (which is a wooden comb), Kachera (which is a special type of under – shorts that we wear), Kara (which is an iron bangle), and the Kirpan (which is a sword).

These objects are not special in themselves, but they represent beliefs and practices that are significant for Sikhs. The turban is not one of the Five Ks, but it is an important outward sign of their faith for Khalsa Sikhs.

'Waheguru Ji Ka Khalsa, Waheguru Ji Ki Fateh' means 'Wonderful Lord's Khalsa, Victory is to the Wonderful Lord.' Sikhs often greet each other with this phrase – reminding themselves of the joy of belonging to the Khalsa, and that this joy is found in God or Waheguru. Anyone who has reached an age of spiritual maturity, male or female, can be initiated into the Khalsa. The first step in joining the Khalsa is taking part in the Amrit ceremony (see Unit 2.6).

Sikhs who choose not to show such a public and physical commitment to their faith often don't wear the Five Ks – but still recognize themselves as Sikhs, although they are non-Khalsa. Many Khalsa Sikhs struggle with this idea, because they believe that the fullest reflection of their faith can only be found by joining the Khalsa.

Reflection

Look back at your response to the starter activity and use the list of words from Activity 2 to explain how it feels to belong.

a Young Sikhs celebrate the establishment of the Khalsa by taking part in Khalsa Day celebrations.

Activities

1 From what you have already learned, and some extra research, explain how a Sikh becomes a member of the Khalsa, showing the meaning of religious symbols and actions.

2 Design a poster from the Khalsa aimed at encouraging non-Khalsa Sikhs to join. You may wish to include words such as identity, commitment, family, faith, belonging and serving.

3 Do some research to find out how people show they belong to other religious communities which you may have studied before. Use the list of words in Activity 2 to help you.

4 Some Khalsa Sikhs believe that non-Khalsa Sikhs are not true Sikhs, although many don't agree with this. Pose questions to explore both points of view.

Learning Objectives

In this unit you will:

- analyse and explain the deeper significance of the Five Ks
- identify issues for Sikhs who wear the signs of their faith
- reflect on your own responses to people who want to show the signs of their faith.

Starter

- What do your clothes and your hairstyle say about you?
- Have you ever judged anyone because of how they look?

Case Study

The Five Ks represent beliefs that are fundamental to the Sikh faith and how it is practised. Balwir Singh has fully adopted the Five Ks into his life, as part of his membership of the Khalsa. Below he explains the importance of their symbolism.

The turban, whilst not strictly named as one of the Five Ks, is a compulsory article of faith that a Sikh wears to cover his or her uncut hair. A turbaned Sikh will never allow his or her turban to be removed, in private or public. Khalsa Sikhs have to accept the challenges of wearing them in today's society.

1 'Kesh – uncut hair. We don't cut it, because it's a gift from God and we respect God.'

2 'Kangha – a wooden comb. We use it to take away dead hair and keeps the hair neat and clean. We keep it in our hair.'

a

3 'Kachera – a type of Sikh under-shorts, to show modesty.'

b

4 'Kara – worn on the right wrist. The Kara stands for truth and for one God without end. It is made from iron or steel so that it doesn't break – indicating that truth is eternal.'

c

5 'Kirpan – a sword. We keep it for defending truth, and not for bad things. it's to defend others.'

d

e In 2012, Jatenderpal Singh Bhuller, a member of the Scots Guards, became the first Sikh to mount guard at Buckingham Palace in a turban. He said: 'I am very proud. The regiment is full of history, as is my religion.'

Case Study

I wear the Five Ks 24/7. The Guru said that God said, keep your Five Ks on you as much as you can, so that is what I am doing now. I used to live up north and had a Kesh when I was little. People used to make fun of me, but I kept the Kesh because – at the end of the day – it's about your religion and how much you love your religion. I could have cut my hair and been like the other kids, but I kept my Kesh and I had love for my God.

Ajit is a non-Khalsa Sikh who has chosen not to wear the Five Ks.

Although I've cut my hair, I still see myself as a Sikh. I try to lead a good life, serve others and honour the Guru Granth Sahib. Those are the things that I think make someone a Sikh. It's about what you're like inside, not what you show on the outside.

? Identify the main points made by Ajit and Balwir. How would you advise a Sikh friend who is thinking about getting his hair cut?

Reflection

Has anyone ever made fun of you because of your appearance? How did it feel?

Activities

1. Explain which of the Five Ks you think would be the easiest to adopt, and which one would be the hardest. Include your reasons.

2. Create a collage of images for each one of the Five Ks – making sure that each image shows something about the meaning of the symbol.

3. How would each of the Five Ks help Balwir Singh practise his faith, as it is described in the Mool Mantar (see Unit 1.1)?

4. How did you feel when you read that people made fun of Balwir because of his hair? What would you say to Balwir if you were one of his friends?

5. In a group, or as a class, produce a debate using the following statement: 'Faith is a private thing and requires no external objects and items.'

3.3 Worship at the Gurdwara

Learning Objectives

In this unit you will:

- explain the role of the gurdwara
- identify the significant elements of worship for a Sikh
- reflect on the extent to which worship is a part of all lives.

Starters

- Close your eyes and sit in complete silence for a few moments. Discuss how it felt to do this.

The focal point for Sikh worship is the gurdwara. 'Gurdwara' means doorway or house of the Guru. The Guru referred to is the holy book, the Guru Granth Sahib (see Unit 2.5). The scriptures are read, and also sung, during Sikh worship. The congregation listens as the **Shabads** are sung to the accompaniment of the tabla (hand drums) and bajas (harmoniums). Sikhs believe that, by singing and listening, they are able to feel the deep vibration of the Gurus' words.

The Guru Granth Sahib is read in the Darbar Sahib, or prayer hall, during times of worship. It is ceremoniously processed from its nightly place of rest, and placed on the **Takht** (covered by a **Palki**). It is then read by a **Granthi**, and the first hymn that he or she reads is called the Hukumnama. The **Chaur** is also waved reverently over the Guru Granth Sahib whilst prayers are being read.

Useful Words

Chaur An implement like a fly whisk that is used to pay respect to the Guru Granth Sahib
Granthi Someone who is fluent in reading the Guru Granth Sahib
Gurbani Teachings of the Guru found in the Guru Granth Sahib and other religious texts
Palki The canopy covering the Guru Granth Sahib
Sangat A Sikh congregation
Shabad The Word of God in Gurbani
Takht The 'throne' on which the Guru Granth Sahib is placed

a

? Why would a Sikh bow to the Guru Granth Sahib? What does this symbolize?

Case Study

Tohmev Singh explains what happens during Sikh worship:

There are two things you do at the gurdwara. One is to join the **sangat**, the holy congregation, in prayer. You can sit and listen to or speak the prayers. The second thing is to do seva (see Unit 3.6).

b Baltej Singh sitting with his parents in a gurdwara.

Men and women sit separately in many gurdwaras, in accordance with cultural practices, and to avoid distractions. However, as Mr Singh explains on the right, everyone is still participating in the worship together.

There is no real significance about whether men are on one side and women are on the other – they all sing the same prayers and they all sit together when they pray, so there is no difference between the genders.

The most important aspect of worship for Tohmev is prayer with the sangat, because it says in the **Gurbani** that Sikhs are lucky to have the holy congregation with them. Mr Singh agrees that worshipping when united with the congregation is very significant. He believes that when the sangat prays, many of the qualities and virtues that he aims for in his daily life can be seen. Worshipping with the sangat also provides the support of being part of a community – which is uplifting.

Reflection

'People worship what they value the most.' Do you agree? What sort of things might that include?

Activities

1. Explain how Sikhs worship in the gurdwara, using at least three of the 'Useful Words'.

2. Why do you think the Guru Granth Sahib is placed on a 'throne' and treated in a special way?

3. Research how the Guru Granth Sahib is used in the home of a Sikh. Compare this with how it is treated in the gurdwara.

4. Why is the time Mr Singh and Tohmev spend in prayer with the sangat the most important part of worship for them? What difference might it make to the way they live their lives? What questions would you like to ask if you met them?

5. You may not worship in a holy building, but ask yourself if there is a place where you devote time to a particular thing/person/ group – a football ground, music venue, art gallery, park, or perhaps even when you are seated around a dining room table. Is some sort of worship part of everybody's life? What advantages are there in having community spaces which people respect?

Learning Objectives

In this unit you will:

- explain the key elements of the Sanskars
- examine the importance of rituals in Sikh life
- reflect on the importance of rituals in your own life.

Starters

- List as many key points of change, or first rituals in your life, as you can. For example, starting school. Why are they memorable?

There are key events in many people's lives that are common, such as the first day at school, or starting your first job. These events – starting with birth and ending with death – are known as rites of passage. For Sikhs, there are a number of significant stages in life. The four most important are known as Sanskars.

Janam Naam Sanskar – the naming ceremony

The birth of a baby is seen as a gift from God. This ceremony happens at the gurdwara, as soon as the mother and baby are able to leave their home. During the ceremony, a randomly chosen verse, or hukam, from the Guru Granth Sahib is read to the family – and the first letter of the first word of the hukam becomes the first letter of the baby's name. If the baby is a boy, the last name 'Singh' (which means 'lion') is also given, and if it's a girl, the last name 'Kaur' ('princess' or 'lioness') is given.

> 'O son, this is your mother's hope and prayer, that you may never forget the Lord, [...] even for an instant.'
> Guru Granth Sahib p.496

Amrit Sanskar – the initiation ceremony

This is a ceremony started by Guru Gobind Singh. It allows a Sikh to join the Khalsa and wear the Five Ks as part of their spiritual journey towards God (see Unit 2.6 for more details about this ceremony).

? The above Shabad was written by Guru Arjan to celebrate the birth of his son, Har Gobind (later the sixth Guru). It is often sung to welcome a new baby. Who chose your name? Does it have any special meaning or significance?

Anand Sanskar – the marriage ceremony

This ceremony means 'blissful' or 'joyful' event, and is seen as much more than simply two people joining together in a legal process. It is the joining of two souls – the unity of the two individual people into one soul, which thinks and feels alike.

> **?** Put this quotation into your own words. Do you agree with this description of marriage?

'The soul-bride is lovingly embellished with truth and contentment; her Father, the Guru, has come to engage her in marriage to her Husband Lord.'
Guru Granth Sahib p.773

Antam Sanskar – the funeral ceremony

Sikhs believe that birth and death are a natural part of life, so death is not to be feared but embraced. Crying or mourning are discouraged at the funeral service, because the soul (the part that does not die) has gone on to the next stage of its journey, which should be celebrated. However, it is not only a celebration of a person's life, but also an acknowledgment that the soul has moved on towards its eventual union with God (see Unit 1.4).

d

Activities

1 a Why do you think Sikhs believe that children are a gift from God?

b Read the Mother's Blessing in the Guru Granth Sahib (p.496), and identify what she's hoping for her child. If you became a parent, what would you wish for your child?

2 Create a congratulations card for someone who has just taken Amrit. What colours would you choose? What would it say inside?

3 Think about the rituals that each human being goes through. If you could, which two rituals would you make sure every single person went through (apart from birth and death)? Give reasons.

> *Reflection*
>
> 'External ceremonies mean nothing if nothing changes inside you.' How would you respond to this comment?

Learning Objectives

In this unit you will:

- explain the role and purpose of celebrating festivals in Sikhism
- identify the impact on Sikhs of celebrating a festival
- explore the values and celebrations within your own local community.

Starter

- What are the ingredients of a good party?

Celebrations in any faith are special, and remind followers of the deeper meaning of their beliefs. Sikhs celebrate a variety of their key beliefs through festivals. Two of the main festivals in Sikhism are Guru Nanak's Gurpurab and Vaisakhi.

Guru Nanak's Gurpurab is the celebration of the anniversary of his birth, which usually falls in the month of November. In India, the Gurpurab is celebrated as a national holiday, and in some schools in the UK it is also school holiday.

Guru Nanak was born in a place which is now called Nanakana Sahib in Pakistan, and Sikhs from all over the world make a special annual visit during the Gurpurab, and grand celebrations are held. Most gurdwaras around the world organize a **Nagar Kirtan**, special hymns are sung, and many exhibit the Sikh martial art of Gatka. The Golden Temple in Amritsar is lit up and fireworks dazzle the night sky.

> **?** See if you can find out more about Guru Nanak's Gurpurab. Why do you think Sikhs celebrate this?

a The Golden Temple at Amritsar, lit up during Guru Nanak's Gurpurab.

b A Sikh procession to mark Guru Nanak's Gurpurab.

Useful Words

Jakara Sikh salutation
Mela A big fair or gathering
Nagar Kirtan A parade led by five Sikhs, to represent the Panj Piare (see Unit 2.6)

Vaisakhi is a festival celebrating the Sikh New Year and the founding of the Khalsa in 1699 (see Unit 2.6).

Why is Vaisakhi so important?

We remember when Guru Gobind Singh created our family (the Khalsa). Vaisakhi weekend is usually around 13 April. We dress up in the colour saffron (to represent the Khalsa) and start by going to the gurdwara first for a blessing from the Guru Granth Sahib.

How do Sikhs celebrate Vaisakhi?

We have **mela** and Nagar Kirtan. This is where Sikhs gather together for a parade with floats and we start from one gurdwara and maybe travel around to another gurdwara, and anyone can join in. It makes you feel as if you are part of a bigger community. It is a get together and it is a happy occasion; everybody is genuinely very happy to see each other and say **jakara**.

What symbols might you see?

To the right is the Nishan Sahib (the Sikh flag). It's got the Sikh emblem on it and is in the saffron Khalsa colours. It shows the Khalsa is here.

c The Nagar Kirtan.

d The Sikh flag.

Activities

1. Do some research and write a diary entry as if you were a Sikh celebrating Vaisakhi.

2. Create a local celebration for all of the things in your community that are important to you. Remember your community isn't always those immediately around you.

3. Why do you think festivals are so important in many faiths? Refer to examples from Hinduism, Judaism, Buddhism and Sikhism.

Reflection

Do people who don't follow a faith miss out on the joys of celebration?

3.6 What is So Important About Seva?

Learning Objectives

In this unit you will:

- explain what seva means and its importance for Sikhs
- analyse the benefits of seva
- reflect on your own feelings about serving others.

Starter

- Write down the different ways in which you are served, or you serve somebody else, in an average day.

Sikhs believe they must carry out seva (or sewa), which is selfless service to God's creation. Therefore, when a Sikh serves others, it is important to remember that he or she is really serving God, as He is in everything He creates. Seva has three parts:

- **Tan** – physical service, e.g. in the free kitchen (the **langar**) at the gurdwara
- **Man** – mental service, such as studying and teaching others
- **Dhan** – giving to charity, or giving time to serve others (see Unit 3.8).

> 'You shall find peace, doing seva [...]
> In the midst of this world, do seva.'
> Guru Granth Sahib p.25–26

b Man – mental service.

a Tan – physical service.

c Dhan – giving time to serve others.

? For each type of service, try to suggest an example of how Sikhs might help their local communities.

Case Study

Baltej Singh explains the important role of the langar as part of seva:

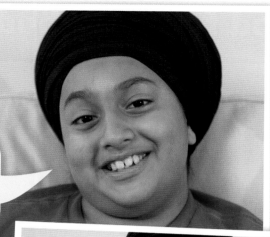

> Some people do seva in the langar. You can help wash the dishes, make the food, or give out the food. Seva makes you feel happy, because you're helping others and doing a good deed. God is pleased with you, and you gain his blessings.

Baltej's mother, Mrs Kaur, adds that the langar is also part of the act of Sikh worship:

> When you do seva, it gives you an opportunity for reflection. When you're doing seva in the kitchen, you and the people you work with are meditating at the same time [**simran**]. We're not gossiping. We may have a little banter, but after that you are meditating in what you are doing – you are remembering God as well, so you are thanking God for the opportunity to go into the kitchen to do seva.

'Meditating, meditating in remembrance, I have found peace.'
Guru Granth Sahib p.202

Useful Words

Langar Both the food and the hall in which it is served, at a gurdwara

Simran Meditating on the word of God; for Sikhs, this must also be completed to balance out seva – to remember God in everything

Reflection

How might the world be a better place if people were less self-centred and more generous?

Activities

1. What does generosity mean? Explain how Sikhs show generosity through the langar.

2. Compare the different types of service shown in the images opposite. Which one do you think would benefit someone the most?

3. Explain how the langar is part of the act of worship for the Sikhs who serve there.

4. As a small group, create a plan for a service that you think you could provide – with no reward – for your local community.

5. Create a design using words, pictures and symbols, around the words of Guru Nanak: 'You shall find peace doing seva', showing the different ways in which Sikhs can serve God and the world.

Learning Objectives

In this unit you will:

- explain the significance of the langar in Sikhism
- interpret the value of sharing and serving for Sikhs
- reflect on ways of giving to your local community.

Starter

- When have you experienced generosity from others? How did it make you feel?

In a gurdwara, you will find a large prayer hall and a kitchen/communal eating hall (the langar hall), which is about the same size. The food and the room where it's served are both called the langar. Mr Singh, Mrs Kaur and Balwir Singh all regularly attend and support their local langar.

Langar is what you will find in any gurdwara — and it's free and open to anybody — so we will have the langar on at lunchtimes and there will always be one in the evening.

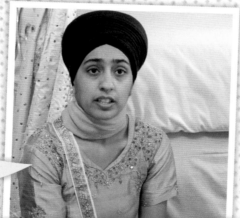

The Langar in the gurdwara is where food is donated through the Sangat. They bring food with them, whether it's milk, lentils, rice, salad — and then what the gurdwara does is create langar.

When Guru Nanak was small, his father gave him 20 rupees and told him to try to get a job, so Guru Nanak went to the town near where he lived. He saw some safoos (some spiritual people). They were very hungry, and hadn't had enough to eat for days, so Guru Nanak thought: 'What if I gave them food today?' So he got his 20 rupees, bought food for them and then they were really happy. [Guru Nanak kept up this generosity, and set in motion the origins of the langar — aiming to feed everyone and anyone, and create equality.]

What impact can the langar have? Sikhs believe that the langar is about more than providing food for those in need. They believe that they have a duty to follow the example and instructions of the Gurus. A belief in equality is at the heart of Sikhism.

? Look at the images on this page. How do they reflect the principles of the langar?

Sometimes you do get people who are homeless who may not have had a meal for a long time; you can see the look of relief that they are actually getting a full meal. It is not our kitchen, it is Guru's kitchen and Guru's kitchen is providing for everybody.

a The langar hall, by artist Jag Lall Singh.

Traditionally, the langar has always been where people sit on the floor and the food is served. It is a sign of equality. They receive the same food and everyone gets it from the same dishes, and we all sit at the same place. It is more about inclusion rather than exclusion.

Reflection

Why is giving and sharing food so important in some faiths?

Activities

1. Create a list of ten words that summarize what the langar does.

2. Read the accounts in this unit carefully. What do you think the speakers get from being part of the langar? What do you think they hope to give to others? Create a word-cloud to show your ideas.

3. **a** The langar takes up as much space in the gurdwara as the prayer hall. What does that tell you about the value that Sikhs place on hospitality and generosity to others?

    b Explain how and why the langar expresses a number of different Sikh beliefs you have studied. Try to identify as many as you can.

4. If you had a party and you were able to invite a whole range of different people, past or present, who would you invite and why? Would you be selective, or would you let anyone come?

5. Imagine if you had the funding to set up a free kitchen in your local community. Where would you put it? Why there? Who would you expect to come along? Who would you be surprised to see?

3.8 Should We Care For Others?

Learning Objectives

In this unit you will:

- explain Sikh teachings about how they should treat others
- examine ways in which Sikhs give their time and money to help those in need
- reflect on your own attitude towards caring for others.

Starters

- Create a mind-map to explore what you believe about giving to those in need.
- Discuss: 'Do we have an obligation to look after one another?'

As you may remember from Unit 1.3, there are three main duties for Sikhs to fulfil. One of them is vand chhakna, which instructs Sikh followers to share their earnings with others and give to charity. Guru Nanak encouraged his followers to give, saying that those who give to charity are 'as pure as the water of the Ganges' (Guru Granth Sahib p.952).

Charitable giving, of both time and money, is known as dhan (see Unit 3.6). It's not about giving to feel or look good. Giving willingly and through honest, honourable means is central to dhan.

Part of this process is the Sikh duty of daswandh, which is to give a tenth of their salary as a charitable donation for the welfare of the local community. This reminds Sikhs that everything comes from God and should be given to serve His people.

However, giving dhan is not only for the rich, because Sikhs can also give their time and skills, as well as their money. Also, the value of the gift should be viewed in the context of the giver's situation – giving someone a simple meal from almost bare cupboards could be seen as more worthy than a rich man providing a feast from overflowing cupboards.

? Should everybody who is able to have a duty to give? Discuss with a partner and create a statement of response.

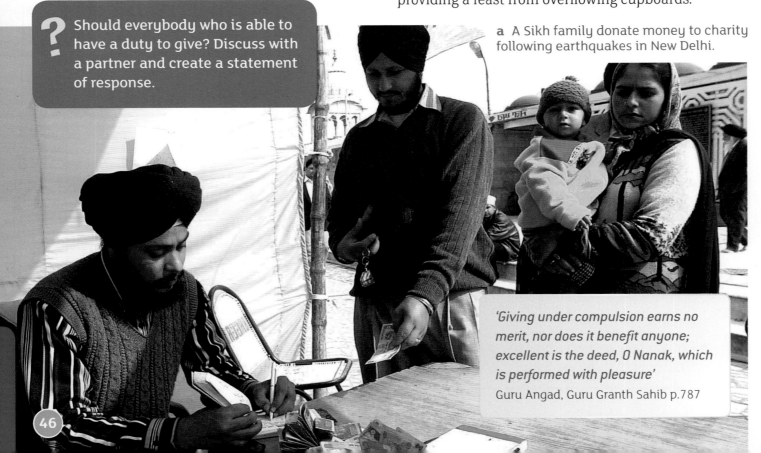

a A Sikh family donate money to charity following earthquakes in New Delhi.

'Giving under compulsion earns no merit, nor does it benefit anyone; excellent is the deed, O Nanak, which is performed with pleasure'
Guru Angad, Guru Granth Sahib p.787

Many Sikhs live by the principles of dhan, and many Sikh organizations put charitable giving at the heart of what they do. For example, Khalsa Aid aims to 'recognize the whole human race as one', and is mainly 'a humanitarian relief agency, based on the teachings of the Sikh Gurus who preached well-being of all humanity' (Khalsa Aid).

This charity gives time, donations and expertise where it's needed. It was started by Ravinder Singh Sidhu, who responded to needs he saw around the world. After asking for help from those around him and beyond, truckloads of aid went out – and Khalsa Aid was born. It has since supported earthquake and tsunami victims, refugees, communities in poverty, and many more. There are currently two main projects in Haiti and the Punjab.

b Khalsa Aid workers providing practical help to earthquake victims in Haiti.

c Khalsa Aid logo.

? Read more about the work that Khalsa Aid has done (http://www.khalsaaid.org/). How is Ravinder Singh Sidhu living up to the name of his charity?

Reflection

'Giving should be a choice, not a duty.' Do you agree? Do you think that people give out of choice or a sense of guilt?

Activities

1 Answer the question in the title of this unit. Explain how far you would go to care for others. Would you give a tenth of the value of the presents you receive on your birthday or any money you are given? Why or why not? Should a Sikh?

2 'Hello world, this is God. Your levels of care for each other show that ...' Looking around at the world today, how do you think God might finish this sentence?

3 Do you think that people would care for others without a belief in God? Explain your answer, referring to the following views:

- 'People need religion to tell them to care for others.'
- 'People are basically good and would look out for others without the need for religion.'
- 'You have a duty to put friends and family first, without needing to worry about strangers.'

Chapter 3 Assessment
Belonging to the Sikh Faith

Objectives

- Explore and explain the ways in which faith can give more to a person than simply something to worship.
- Reflect on your own ideas about where guidance and direction can come from in life.

Task

Your task is to write a letter from a parent to a teenager, aged around 13–14, who is getting ready to join the Khalsa by having an Amrit ceremony. In the letter, explain:

- why the Khalsa is so important
- what it can give a Sikh in terms of support and guidance
- how the Five Ks can make a big difference to a Sikh's life.

Also refer to the greater responsibilities that the teenager will now have – especially in terms of seva and their own worship in the gurdwara.

A bit of guidance...

Remember that this is a parent writing to their child, so make it caring (not really formal or full of instruction). Sikhs love their faith and find joy in practising it, so try to get that across, too.

Hints and tips

To help you tackle this task, you could:

- Try to use some key words from this chapter – choose at least five to include
- Remind yourself about Sikh perspectives by looking back over the case study sections in this chapter
- Aim to include examples of how the parent might have found belonging to the Khalsa, and performing seva, both helpful and a challenge to them – allowing them to grow in their faith and beliefs

a

	I can...
Level 3	• describe what a believer might learn from a religious story or teaching • ask important questions about Sikhism and Sikh beliefs about God – making links between my own responses and those of others.
Level 4	• make links between the beliefs of a religious group and how they are connected to believers' lives • raise and suggest answers to questions of identity, meaning, belonging, purpose and truth.
Level 5	• use a wide range of religious vocabulary to explain the impact of Sikh belief in God on individuals and communities • ask questions and suggest answers to important questions about meaning and morality.
Level 6	• give an account of the variety of religious responses to questions of belief, and explain why they are different • give my views about the important questions, with reasons and examples, and show how following religious teachings might be a challenge in the modern world.

Ready for more?

When you have completed this task, you can also work on your skills for Levels 6 and 7, and perhaps even higher. This is an extension task.

Write a response from the Sikh teenager to the parent, explaining what you are looking forward to and anything that might be worrying you.

• Try to show a range of emotions and expectations.

• Use key vocabulary.

• Demonstrate understanding of the important elements found in this chapter.

4.1 A Question of Money

Learning Objectives

In this unit you will:

- examine the story of Duni Chand and the lesson it offers for Sikhs
- explore the role of wealth and the desire for it in the modern world
- reflect on your own approach to money.

Starter

- If you had to choose one, what would you rather be: rich or happy? Discuss with a partner.

The Story of Duni Chand

There once was a very rich man called Duni Chand, whose only goal in life was to be the richest person he knew. He kept symbols of his wealth all around his property and when Guru Nanak (see Units 2.1 and 2.2) came into town, Duni Chand invited him to his house to show off his wealth.

Guru Nanak did something a little odd though. Instead of being impressed by his riches, the Guru asked Duni Chand to look after a small needle, and to give it back to him in the next life.

a Duni Chand with the needle from Guru Nanak.

What do you think the end to the story is? Does it sound as though there might be a moral to this story?

? Read the quotations carefully. What are the challenges to Sikhs living in a society that values wealth and material possessions? How might a Sikh feel if they successfully let go of their attachments?

'People fall in love with the shade of the tree, and when it passes away, they feel regret in their minds. Whatever is seen, shall pass away; and yet, the blindest of the blind cling to it.'
Guru Granth Sahib p.268

'False are body, wealth, and all relations. False are ego, possessiveness [...] False are power, youth, wealth and property. [...] False are chariots, elephants, horses and expensive clothes. False is the love of gathering wealth, and revelling in the sight of it.'
Guru Granth Sahib p.268

After Guru Nanak had gone, Duni Chand went to his wife and told her what the Guru had asked him to do. She pointed out that it was impossible to take anything into the next life and to return the needle straight away. Duni Chand returned the needle to the Guru, who said, 'If such a small and light thing as a needle cannot go to the next world, how can your wealth reach there?'

? Pick one of the following questions to discuss with a partner: Why are some people so obsessed with having lots of money? Is there such a thing as having 'too much money'? How far would you go for great riches?

So why was the needle given to Duni Chand in the first place? The Guru asked Duni Chand to take the needle into the next life for a specific reason, and that was to show him that life is temporary – nothing lasts forever, not even his wealth. Instead, he should give it all up and build his spiritual wealth by giving to and caring for the poor.

? What would Duni Chand have said to these people before Guru Nanak's visit, and how would he have changed after the Guru's visit?

Reflection

Guru Nanak helped Duni Chand as a result of him asking the Guru to visit him at his house. Do you think you should help others only when they ask you for help? Why or why not?

Activities

1 Choose five key words from the story of Duni Chand, and explain in your own words the meaning of the story.

2 🖥 📄 A little imagination needed now: create a large outline of a needle and within it, put all the images that you think represent what Duni Chand was trying to hold onto. Use the photos above as a starting point.

3 How could a modern Sikh put this story into practice in their life?

4 Which of your possessions would you find it hardest to let go, and why?

5 Guru Nanak said, 'Cursed is the life which is lived only to fatten one's belly'. Do you think money brings true happiness, or is life about something more than wealth? If so, what is that 'something'? Discuss this with a partner or explain your ideas in your notes.

4.2 Our Environment: Living in Harmony

Learning Objectives

In this unit you will:

- explain Sikh beliefs about the relationship between humans and the environment
- identify some environmental ethical issues and how Sikhs respond to them
- reflect on taking responsibility for the environment.

Starter

- How much do you care about saving the environment? What do you do?

Sikhs believe that God created the natural world and humans – and that, therefore, there is a sacred relationship between humans and the environment. Humans should try to be in **harmony** with God's creation, and protect this sacred relationship. The Gurus taught that humans have a responsibility towards their environment, and that they should respect all that it gives them. Some Sikhs use the term 'eco-sophism', which means wisdom of the universe. This teaches Sikhs to be aware of what is best for the universe and its protection.

Useful Words

Biodiversity The variety of life in a particular place
Harmony Agreement in thought and deed
Sustainable Able to be maintained

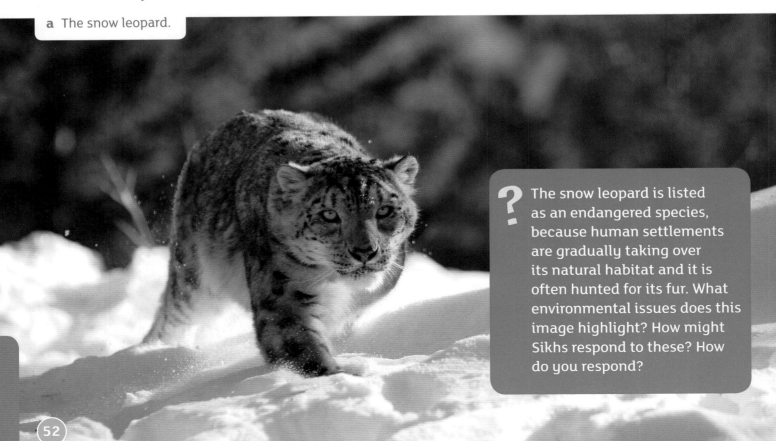

a The snow leopard.

? The snow leopard is listed as an endangered species, because human settlements are gradually taking over its natural habitat and it is often hunted for its fur. What environmental issues does this image highlight? How might Sikhs respond to these? How do you respond?

The number of environmental problems has grown over the past few decades. Global warming and its consequences; the extinction of many plant and animal species; air, ground and water pollution; and the rapid reduction of finite resources, such as coal and oil, are all issues having an impact on how people live their lives and the choices they make. Sikhs are deeply concerned about these problems – particularly because they believe that it is God's creation that is being affected.

Since 2011, Sikhs all over the world have been celebrating 14 March as Sikh Environment Day. This day was chosen because it marks the anniversary of the enthronement of Guru Har Rai, who was known for his care of plants and animals (see Unit 2.4). Sikh businesses, schools, gurdwaras, and even Sikhs in the British Army, celebrate this day by taking positive steps to protect the environment. For example, the community of the Guru Tegh Bahadur Gurdwara in Leicester chose that day to switch over to solar energy.

EcoSikh

'We honour our Gurus' wisdom by believing that all humans have an intrinsic sensitivity to the natural world, and that a **sustainable**, more just society is possible, where water, air, land, forests and **biodiversity** remain vibrant, living systems for our generation and future generations.'
From the EcoSikh website
http://www.ecosikh.org

? Try to put the quotation above from EcoSikh (an environmental charity) into your own words. If you are not sure, pair up with someone and share your ideas.

b A gurdwara in Leicester switches to solar energy.

Reflection

Our world will become the world of future generations. Do we have a responsibility to look after it, or should we leave it up to them? Explain the reasons for your opinion.

Activities

1 Design a flier to go to Year 2 and 3 students, telling them what Sikhs believe about the environment.

2 Create a role-play of an argument between someone who doesn't care about the environment and a Sikh who cares deeply. Ask the class to decide who wins.

3 Write a local radio report about the switch to solar energy at the Leicester Gurdwara. Include interviews with members of the Sikh community to explain why they did it and how their actions reflect Sikh beliefs.

4.3 Sikhism and Science: United or Divided?

Learning Objectives

In this unit you will:

- examine the relationship between Sikhism and science
- compare the approaches of a Sikh and a scientist to our universe
- reflect on where you stand in terms of these two approaches.

Starter

- What do you know about the beginning of our universe?

Case Study

Mejindarpal Kaur is the Legal Director of UNITED SIKHS, an international UN associated advocacy charity. She believes there are clear links between Sikhism and science.

> There are many who would argue that science and religion are in constant conflict, since faiths usually believe that a god is in control of the universe, while scientific theories about the origins of the universe contradict this. But this is not the case for many Sikhs.

> *'You created the vast expanse of the Universe with One Word!'*
> Guru Granth Sahib p.3

> Truth has to be consistent. The **Big Bang** theory is based on there being one moment when the universe was created, and the Guru Granth Sahib suggests to us that creation was through one command, which means there was a moment when it was created.

'Big Bang happened by chance' — 'God created the universe – it has nothing to do with the Big Bang'

a Where would you place yourself on this line? Explain to a partner the reasons why.

Useful Words

Big Bang A scientific theory that suggests the universe began billions of years ago by a massive explosion of dense matter, which caused all forms of planets, stars and life to begin developing

Gurmukhs Those who follow in the Gurus' teachings

Case Study

Sikhs believe that only God knows exactly what happened at the start of the universe since only he was there. Science can help people to understand as much as possible about the earth and the galaxies beyond, but, as Ms Kaur explained, since scientists are searching for the truth, and faith is also about seeking the truth (see the quotations from the Guru Granth Sahib), then many Sikhs believe that science and religion should not be in conflict with each other.

If someone is misguided about what truth is, or science is making mistakes because someone has badly researched something, then you might see inconsistencies [… but] if Sikhism and all faiths are taking [humans] towards the truth, then, at the end of the day, there should be no inconsistency.

'What was that season, and what was that month, when the Universe was created? […]The Creator who created this creation – only He Himself knows.'
Guru Granth Sahib p.4

'Many millions are created in various forms. From God they emanate, and into God they merge once again. His limits are not known to anyone.'
Guru Granth Sahib p.276

'One Universal Creator God. The Name is Truth. […]True in the Primal Beginning. True Throughout the Ages. True Here and Now. O Nanak, Forever and Ever True.'
Guru Granth Sahib p.1

? Note down the key beliefs that these quotations put forward. How could they inform a debate about the relationship between Sikhism and science?

Reflection
Does the belief that there is a creator give this world a purpose?

Activities

1. Create a poster or image that represents the belief that God created the whole world with one single command. How would the beginning look like? What would that one command be? Use your creativity.

2. Some Sikhs, like Ms Kaur, believe that the Big Bang theory is consistent with the one moment of creation that Sikhs believe in. What do you think? Discuss your reasons with a partner.

3. For Sikhs, both science and religion are about finding the truth. For Humanists, science provides the only reliable source of knowledge about the origins of life. Using the quotations above, write a short email from a Sikh to a Humanist friend explaining how it is possible to believe in both science and religion.

Learning Objectives

In this unit we will:

- explain Sikh attitudes towards **abortion**
- analyse Sikh teaching about the sanctity of human life
- reflect on your own views about the issues raised.

Starters

- What medical ethical issues do you already know about?
- Work with a partner to list as many arguments about medical ethics as you can.

Medical ethics involves deciding what is right and wrong when giving care and treatment that may save or end a life. Medical knowledge and skills have developed significantly, and it is now possible to do more and more to keep people fit, healthy and alive. It is also possible to choose to end a life. For example, abortion involves the medical ending of a pregnancy at an early stage. Making such life and death decisions is very difficult. People who hold religious beliefs often have very strong views about these issues.

Is life **sacred**? Sikhs believe that all life begins at **conception**, and that the divine spark of God is in everyone – for He is the creator of all living things. They also believe in following hukam, or God's will – and that He is the only one who can be in control of the birth and death of humans. Sikhs believe that destroying the life of a foetus by abortion is to destroy a sacred life with the essence of God within it. Abortion is only acceptable if the mother's life is at risk.

To Sikhs, any form of treatment or procedure that involves changing, starting or ending life contrary to the way it was intended by God is unacceptable. This means that a number of issues, such as abortion, **embryo testing**, and **euthanasia** raise difficult questions for Sikhs.

> '*O, my body, God infused divine light in you and you were born into the world.*'
> Guru Granth Sahib p.921
>
> '*God sends us and we take birth. God calls us back and we die.*'
> Guru Granth Sahib p.1239

? Read through the Sikh attitudes toward the sanctity of life, and then put the two quotations above into your own words. Try applying this to one of the ethical issues mentioned on this page. What would a Sikh not be able to do?

a A British Sikh family with a newly born baby.

Some believe that abortion is no different from murder, whilst others believe it is the woman's right to choose to end the life of her foetus at any stage of the pregnancy. Many others would position themselves somewhere between these two viewpoints. A key question is: when does human life actually begin? Does it begin at conception, as Sikhs would argue, or later?

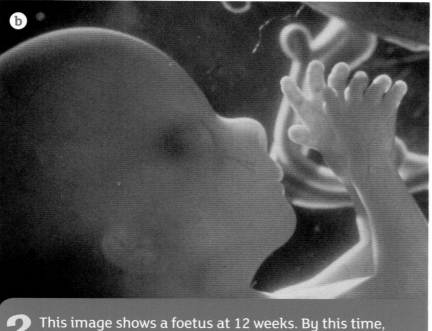

? This image shows a foetus at 12 weeks. By this time, the foetus has developed nearly all of its organs, as well as facial features, fingers and toes. Do some research to find out the key milestones in the development of a foetus. Then discuss with a partner: at what point in the development process does life begin?

? Write a letter to a 16-year-old girl (or boy) who is expecting a baby, and suggest what they should do and why they should do it. Make sure you refer to different arguments, including Sikh views.

Useful Words

Abortion Medically removing a baby from the womb during pregnancy

Conception The moment that a sperm fertilizes an egg and a woman becomes pregnant

Embryo testing Scientific testing on a foetus at very early stages of development, usually for medical research

Euthanasia Helping someone else to die

Sacred Holy, or a gift from God

Reflection

What are the potential dangers of humans 'playing God'?

Activities

1 Summarize the approach that most Sikhs take on matters of life and death, such as abortion and euthanasia, using all of the 'Useful Words' listed.

2 In pairs, create a speech that aims to convince the listener that the Sikh approach towards matters of life and death is the approach that everyone should take. Identify the main arguments that you are going to use before you start writing.

3 Research how a Humanist or member of another faith might respond to these issues and, using a method of your choice, write up your findings to compare them with Sikhism.

4 Prepare your arguments for a class debate on the statement: 'The belief that there is the essence of God in all life makes accepting abortion impossible.'

Raising Questions, Exploring Answers   57

Learning Objectives

In this unit you will:

- explain Sikh attitudes to **IVF** and **cloning**
- analyse Sikh teachings about the sanctity of human life
- reflect on your own views about the issues raised.

Starter

- If you could choose certain things about your future child, such as gender or hair colour, would you?

The Guru Granth Sahib does not make reference to modern medical ethical issues. However, Sikhs base their decisions on interpreting the Guru Granth Sahib, which says that everything in this world is God's creation. Therefore, anything created on earth by people is also created by God, and is within His will. For Sikhs, medical ethical issues can be both clear-cut and complicated.

Our religion is very much at the forefront of everything we do. We have to consider: 'Is this the right thing to do? Does it go with the Gurus' teachings?' If it does, no problem.

If you keep going back to the holy Sikh scripture of the Guru Granth Sahib for guidance, I am sure you will always find [answers] there, if you look […] and ask, what have I learned from the Guru Granth Sahib?

One issue that Sikhs might find it difficult to make a decision about is in-vitro fertilization, or IVF. Mrs Kaur explains that, if there is no testing or destruction of cells, IVF can be acceptable. However, her nephew Tohmev adds that, if you end up with too many embryos (more than you need), there will be a problem:

They throw away all the rest [of the embryos] and they kill them. We believe that is wrong, because we believe that — as soon as conception has taken place — that being has got a soul.

? There is a strong emphasis on children and family life in Sikhism, and it is difficult for a couple who are unable to conceive to accept that this is the will of God. Why would this be difficult?

Two other questions of medical ethics that present problems for Sikhs are the use of animals for medical research (for example, testing new drugs or cosmetics on them), and cloning. Mrs Kaur and Mr Singh discuss these two issues.

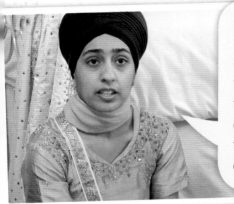

> In every creation there is a soul. We don't agree with causing anything to suffer for us. We may be in pain, but there is no reason why God can't ease the pain, rather than using an animal to create a product.

Mr Singh then considers cloning, arguing:

> We believe that everything has a soul; the soul is separated from God. Our purpose of being here […] is to join back with God.

So, if animals are cloned, does this mean that they don't have a soul and can't return to God? Sikhs don't believe that anything can live without a soul. Therefore, a cloned animal must have a soul if it's alive. Mr Singh adds that cloning may be another way in which the Creator works, and so may be acceptable.

? Create a ten-word sentence that summarizes the Sikh attitude towards animal testing. Discuss how you feel about cloning with a partner. Compare your responses with those of Mr Singh.

Useful Words

Cloning Cultivating DNA to make an exact copy of a living creature
IVF In-vitro fertilization; this treatment helps couples to have children by fertilizing the egg outside the womb and then implanting it back into the woman

Reflection

Do you believe that every human and every animal has a soul? Why or why not?

Activities

1. Research and explain what having IVF involves and the issues it raises.

2. **a** Consider the idea that medical scientific processes (such as cloning) might be 'another way in which the Creator works'. How would this help Sikhs to make ethical decisions?
   b How does the belief that everything has a soul, which will eventually return to God, affect how Sikhs view animal testing and cloning?

3. Is having a child something that everyone has the right to do? List the arguments for and against.

4. 'Medical developments should be limited. We don't know the consequences of what we are doing.' Discuss with a partner.

Friends? Relationships? Marriage?

Learning Objectives

In this unit you will:

- explain how some Sikhs view friendships
- analyse Sikh attitudes towards marriage
- reflect on your own friendships and the relationships around you.

Starter

- What guidance have you been given, if any, about who you can be in a relationship with?

What do Sikhs believe about friendships and relationships? Mr Singh and his wife, Mrs Kaur, explain:

I think friends are very important. Each friend has unique qualities that you can learn from, and they bring different aspects to your relationship. The advantage of having Sikh friends is that you can pray together and sing praises in congregation, which is very important as a Sikh.

A friend is good if they remind you about God. You get it from their presence, you feel calmer, happier; traits which help us become closer to God as well.

Unlike some Western behaviours, initiated Sikhs do not go looking for romantic friendships:

Sikhs who are initiated go into a relationship with the intention of marriage. You don't go out looking for a relationship in the hope of starting to date. You don't go down the route of having a relationship and moving on from another to another. There is already somebody ordained by God to be your life partner, so you look at everybody as your sister or brother, or your aunt or uncle, and you treat them with due respect.

? Do you think there is someone 'out there' who is meant to be for you? Why or why not?

Guru Nanak stressed the importance of marriage, so all Sikhs are encouraged to marry. Marriage is seen as a spiritual union between two equal partners:

> As initiated Sikhs, the relationship that we are trying to build up is with God, so the focus is on going down that path. That is the hope that we have for our children. We teach them that there is somebody that they are going to get married to, and we will leave that up to God.

For Sikhs, marriage is a commitment before God. Marriage can be described as 'one soul in two bodies', so being faithful to a husband or wife is central to Sikh life.

During a Sikh wedding, the couple walk four times clockwise around the Guru Granth Sahib, linked together by a length of cloth (showing that the scriptures are what unites them). Lavan, which are four hymns composed by Guru Ram Das, are read first, then sung, during the couple's walk around the Guru Granth Sahib.

'In the first round of the marriage ceremony, the Lord sets out His Instructions for performing the daily duties of married life.
In the second round of the marriage ceremony, the Lord leads you to meet the True Guru, the Primal Being.
In the third round of the marriage ceremony, the mind is filled with Divine Love.
In the fourth round of the marriage ceremony, my mind has become peaceful; I have found the Lord.'

From the Four Lavan, Guru Granth Sahib, p.773–774

? What do the Lavan suggest should be at the heart of a Sikh marriage? What do you think should be at the heart of a marriage?

Reflection

'It's okay to be single. You don't need another person to complete you.' How would you respond to this statement?

Activities

1. Imagine that you have attended the wedding of a Sikh friend. Write a letter/postcard/email to another friend explaining what happened and the significance of the words and actions.

2. How important is it that a person should choose to marry someone who shares their beliefs – religious or otherwise? Explain your thoughts.

3. Marriage is not as important to some people as it used to be. What do you think a Sikh would say in response to this?

4. • 'The more people you date, the more likely you are to find the perfect life partner.'
   • 'If you treat finding a partner like trying different clothes on for size in the shops, then you will never understand what marriage is really about.'

   Consider these two views. What do you think? How might a Sikh respond?

Raising Questions, Exploring Answers

Objectives

- Explore some key questions and issues of the modern world, and identify and analyse some Sikh responses to them.
- Show understanding and awareness of significant issues in the modern world.

Task

'Religion cannot give any guidance on how to live in the modern world.' Respond to this statement from the point of view of a young Sikh living in the UK today.

Write at least three paragraphs in response to the above quotation. Make sure you include something about the challenges that a young Sikh would face when trying to put their faith into practice in today's world.

a

A bit of guidance...

Look back over the different issues you have covered in this unit, such as wealth, the environment and medical ethics. Consider whether or not religion, in this case Sikhism, can offer any guidance for these modern issues.

Hints and tips

To help you tackle this task, you could include some of the following:

- Guru Nanak's teaching on money and wealth
- How Sikhs respond to environmental or medical issues
- Developments in science and Sikh responses to them
- Beliefs about relationships and marriage.

Guidance

What level are you aiming at? Have a look at the grid below to see what you need to do to achieve that level. What would you need to do to improve your work?

I can...	
Level 3	• describe what a believer might learn from a religious story or teaching • make links between beliefs and values, and my own and others' behaviours.
Level 4	• make links between the beliefs of a religious group and how they are connected to believers' lives • ask questions about identity and belonging, and apply them to my own and others' lives.
Level 5	• explain how religious teachings are used to provide answers to important questions about behaviour and morality • ask questions, and suggest answers to important questions about meaning and morality.
Level 6	• give an account of the variety of religious responses to questions of belief, explaining why they are different • give my viewpoint on the important questions, giving reasons and examples, and show how following religious teachings might be a challenge in the modern world.

ⓑ

Ready for more?

When you have completed this task, you can also work on your skills for Levels 6 and 7, and perhaps even higher. This is an extension task.

Your task now is to respond to the statement from your own point of view. Do you agree or disagree? Compare and contrast your own views with those of a young Sikh's. Make sure to describe any similarities or differences between the two perspectives.

5.1 Fighting For Justice

Learning Objectives

In this unit you will:

- explain the significance of the story of Guru Har Gobind
- evaluate the work of UNITED SIKHS
- reflect on what it takes to fight injustice.

Starter

- Look at the four people pictured below. Who are they? What do they have in common?

What would you be prepared to do for your beliefs? The four people pictured on the right were all imprisoned for standing up against injustice. Sikhs believe that they should fight for the rights of others, and also recognize that they have a responsibility to support those in need. The two side swords on the Khanda symbol represent both spiritual authority and the fight against injustice in the world (see Unit 1.3).

Guru Har Gobind believed in fighting against **injustice**, and for those who could not fight for themselves. The Mogul Emperor, Jahangir, imprisoned him unjustly for over two years, along with other **political prisoners**. Guru Har Gobind shared his food with them, prayed with them, and kept their spirits up. He said: 'The ruler can imprison my body but my mind cannot be imprisoned'.

When his freedom was eventually negotiated, the Guru refused to leave unless the other prisoners were released with him – emphasizing the importance he placed on righteousness and **justice**, and showing real **altruism**. To limit the number of prisoners who could leave, the Emperor agreed that he could take whoever could grasp the skirt of his robe. However, when the gates were opened, all 52 of his fellow prisoners left with him by holding strings which Guru Har Gobind had sewn into his clothing.

a

b

c

d

Useful Words

Altruism Selfless care and concern for others
Injustice Violation of the rights of others
Justice Moral righteousness
Political prisoners People imprisoned for their political beliefs or actions

UNITED SIKHS (www.unitedsikhs.org) is an international UN associated charity that works to transform communities and individuals into vibrant members of society through advocacy, education and personal development programmes.

Mejindarpal Kaur says: *'In recent years, we have seen a ban against the wearing of religious signs in schools, particularly in France and Belgium. We see this as an attack on religious freedom. Since 2004, Sikh school children in France and recently in Belgium have had to go to school bare-headed against their religious mandate to keep their unshorn hair covered with a turban or patka (scarf). This ban has also affected Jewish, Christian and Muslim students.'*

In 2012, with the help of UNITED SIKHS lawyers, a French Sikh student, Bikramjit Singh, won a case before the United Nations Human Rights Committee (UNHRC) for the right to wear signs of his faith at school. Sikhs believe this victory is a first step that will one day benefit all religious communities in France. Guru Har Gobind fought for this same principle – fighting a battle so others may know freedom in their lives.

e

UNITED SIKHS
Recognize the Human Race as One

f UNITED SIKHS peacefully protest in France.

> **?** What do you think about people wearing signs of their faith to school?

Activities

1. Choose five key words and use them to sum up the actions of Guru Har Gobind.

2. What do you think Guru Har Gobind meant when he said 'The ruler can imprison my body but my mind cannot be imprisoned'? How might his words give hope to people who have been unjustly imprisoned?

3. Role-play, with a partner, an interview with Guru Har Gobind, following his release from prison, for a TV programme about fighting for justice.

4. Do some research to find out why Terry Waite, Nelson Mandela and Aung San Suu Kyi were imprisoned. In each case, identify their key beliefs.

5. 'It's impossible to be truly altruistic.' Discuss this statement with a partner (with particular reference to Guru Har Gobind and the other prisoners you have researched).

Reflection
Do you think you have a responsibility to help people you don't know?

Learning Objectives

In this unit you will:

- evaluate the importance of history to Sikhs
- explain the significance of the events at Amritsar in 1984
- consider what you would do if faced with a life-or-death situation.

The Golden Temple at Amritsar, India, is one of the holiest places for Sikhs (see Unit 2.3). However, in 1919 (during the period of British rule over India), a terrible massacre took place a few hundred yards away. The British Governor of the area, General Dyer, ordered his troops to open fire without warning on a crowd of over 10,000 unarmed Sikh pilgrims and others, killing 379 and injuring 1,200. In February 2013, the British Prime Minister David Cameron visited the memorial at the site of the massacre. Writing in the Book of Condolences, he described the massacre as a 'deeply shameful event in British history', adding that 'we must never forget what happened here'.

When India became independent in 1947, Sikhs wanted their own state, and Jawaharlal Nehru, who was leading the Independence talks with Britain, said of the Sikh demand: 'I see nothing wrong in an area and a set up in the North wherein the Sikhs can also experience the glow of freedom.' However, after Independence, this promise was broken, which unsettled a number of Sikhs even decades after.

One Sikh leader, Jarnail Singh Bhindranwale, took action. In 1983, he led a group of Sikhs who barricaded themselves in the complex at the Golden Temple — protesting at the lack of freedom and rights given to Sikhs. In June 1984, after various attempts to resolve the situation, Indian troops launched an attack under the order of Indira Gandhi, the Indian Prime Minister at that time. She was the daughter of Jawaharlal Nehru. They attacked the Temple complex, damaged the holy site, and killed thousands of innocent pilgrims who were there for the martyrdom anniversary of Guru Arjan.

? Do you feel so strongly about something that you would be prepared to fight, perhaps to the death, for it? Consider the idea of dying for a belief, and the reasons that people might give for and against the idea.

a Britain's Prime Minister David Cameron visits the Golden Temple in February 2013 to lay a memorial wreath.

b The Golden Temple at Amritsar, severely damaged after the 1984 attacks.

Unfortunately, the situation did not end there. A great deal of sorrow was felt in the Sikh community as result of the attack, and the anger was so great that two Sikh bodyguards of the Indian Prime Minister, Indira Gandhi, assassinated her. Anti-Sikh violence followed and reports from the time suggest that over 10,000 Sikhs were killed. In April 2013, a Delhi court judge hearing a case of killings in November 1984 said that the police remained a silent spectator as the mobsters killed innocent Sikhs. Some 30 years later, Sikhs feel that the main perpetrators of the violence have not been brought to justice, and many feel that, because of this, it is not possible to forgive and forget.

> This is part of our shared history and identity as Sikhs. However, we need to forgive, move on, and learn from what happened.

> Sikhs were victims of violence, but assassination is never the answer. We must accept our share of the responsibility.

> Broken promises are to blame for the events at Amritsar. Sikhs have been wronged and deserve justice.

c Indira Gandhi, Prime Minister of India between 1966–77 and 1980–84.

? The above beliefs express a range of responses to the loss of life in 1984. If you were a Sikh, which belief do you think you would be most likely to agree with?

? Indira Gandhi once said: 'If I die today, every drop of my blood will invigorate the nation.' Can violence ever bring peace, or does it only bring more violence?

Reflection

'History is history. There is no point in looking backwards, only forwards.' What do you think? Explain your response as part of a class discussion.

Activities

1 Explain (in no more than 30 words) why some Sikhs want to remember the events outlined in this unit.

2 What might Sikh values and beliefs 'say' about these events?

3 Uniting in belief brings many people together. Identify two events in history that have united large groups of people. Then create a diagram to show how events unfolded.

4 Create an online news story as if the event were 'Breaking News' today. What would you focus on? Who would you try to get quotes from? Make sure there is no bias in your story.

5 'Religion is always going to produce conflict.' Create four bullet points to both support and reject this claim.

Learning Objectives

In this unit you will:

- identify and analyse the range of responses to the death penalty within Sikhism
- explain why the death penalty is an ethical issue
- consider your own views about the death penalty.

Starter

- Which countries have the death penalty?
- List one argument for and one argument against the death penalty.

Death penalty is the legalized killing of a criminal by the government of a country. Many countries worldwide use the death penalty, including China, Iran, Thailand, Indonesia, certain states in the USA, and India, where the vast majority of the world's Sikhs live.

The crimes of those on **death row** vary, but people are usually there as the result of committing murder. The death penalty is used in a number of ways: as punishment for a crime, as a **deterrent**, and to protect society from criminals. Ultimately, each country's justice system makes the decision about who receives the death penalty. Many people argue that it's **inhumane** and should be illegal, whilst others argue that it's necessary.

One of the key principles of Sikhism is to protect life, so most Sikhs are against the death penalty, because it's seen as killing in cold blood (although some see it as a way of protecting society).

Useful Words

Death row The part of a prison housing those sentenced to death
Deterrent To deter or put others off from committing a crime
Inhumane Cruel; lacking compassion
Nishan Sahib The Sikh flag
Persecution Persistent ill-treatment, usually because of race or religion

a Sikhs protest against Balwant Singh Rajoana's death sentence.

> **?** Why do you think the death penalty is such a controversial issue?

As you saw in Unit 5.2, there was a violent attack by Indian forces on the Golden Temple at Amritsar in 1984. In the years that followed, Sikhs made many claims about **persecution** by the Indian government – and it's alleged that around 25,000 Sikhs disappeared, or were killed, during the time of the Chief Minister of the Punjab, Beant Singh.

In 1995, Beant Singh was killed by a suicide bomber. The bomber was Dilawar Singh, but another Sikh (Balwant Singh Rajoana) later confessed that, had Dilawar not been successful, he was to be the back-up bomber. Balwant Singh Rajoana has spent more than 17 years in custody and was due to be executed in March 2012, when a petition was filed for stay of his execution.

Balwir Singh, along with many Sikhs worldwide, supports his release – believing that Balwant Singh Rajoana has served his punishment. Balwir argues that he is not guilty of a crime that deserves the death penalty and, as a sign of respect for Rajoana, he puts the **Nishan Sahib** up in his home.

? What could a Sikh take from the Mool Mantar (see Unit 1.1) to help them with the issue of death penalty? Explain your choice.

b The Sikh flag.

Reflection

'Only God or chance should take life. No human should do it, for any reason.' Do you agree?

Activities

1 a Using only 20 words, explain the general Sikh attitude towards the death penalty.

 b How could the idea of hukam (God's will) and the words of the Mool Mantar also help?

2 What do you think is the most important aim of punishment? Why?

3 Do you think that the death penalty is justifiable? To what extent would you agree with what most Sikhs think?

4 Some Sikhs are involved in protesting against the death penalty, particularly in India. Do you think that religions should be involved in protesting about political issues?

5.4 Is Equality the Norm?

Learning Objectives

In this unit you will:

- explain Sikh beliefs about the roles of men and women
- apply the teachings of key Gurus to modern Sikh families
- consider where you stand on the issue of equality.

Starter

- Do you believe that men and women are, or should be, equal?
- Do you think that modern society allows men and women to be equal?

At the heart of Sikhism, and throughout the teachings of the Gurus, runs a thread of belief that everyone is equal — regardless of gender, faith, race, or age. This principle of equality began with Guru Nanak and is taught in gurdwaras across the world. Sikhs believe that God created everyone, and that everyone can enter into a relationship with him.

? Look back over the work you did on the Sikh Gurus (Units 2.3 and 2.4). Choose, from any of the Gurus, four key teachings or actions that show they fought for equality.

Case Study

Ms Kaur, legal director of UNITED SIKHS, answers questions on equality in her faith:

Who do you admire?

The Sangat (the Sikh community). They have the qualities that help us to see God in everyone.

What does Sikhism teach about equality? Is there one particular Guru who taught this?

The Guru Granth Sahib starts with the word Ik — which means One. Through the belief in One, we see equality in all, because we see One in all. This equality through the One was taught by all the Gurus.

Are there any other people you admire?

I admire all creation, because I see the Creator in His creation and see the God-qualities in all.

Case Study

The question of equality between men and women has been asked many times across many faiths. How does Sikhism respond to this question? Mejindarpal Kaur explores these ideas:

A Sikh woman and man, or boy and girl, have equal rights in the practice of the faith. For example, a Sikh man or woman may lead prayer, and also partake in Amrit and wear the Five Ks, plus the turban. In a Sikh home, a daughter and son have equal right to education or property. Amongst young people, a Sikh woman has the same freedoms as a Sikh man in choosing her career, and so on. Children are taught respect, duty and love towards their parents. To illustrate this point, in the Guru Granth Sahib there are hymns that refer to God as being a mother and father.

'From woman, man is born; within woman, man is conceived; to woman he is engaged and married. […]
So why call her bad? From her, kings are born.
From woman, woman is born; without woman, there would be no one at all.'
Guru Granth Sahib p.473

? What does the quotation tell us about the value placed upon women in Sikh teachings?

Reflection

In Britain the right for all women to vote was only won in 1928. What do you think about this? Find out which countries still do not allow women to vote.

Activities

1 Summarize, in your own words, what many Sikhs believe about the roles of men and women.

2 Look carefully at what you have written for the above question. Is this what you understand equality to mean? Why or why not?

3 What do you think the qualities of a God who was both father and mother would be?

4 Do you think that equality means being able to do exactly the same as each other with exactly the same skills and opportunities?

5 Design a symbol for man and a symbol for woman that reflect Sikh beliefs.

6 Hold a class or group debate, using the following statement: 'Being equal means that your roles are valued equally.'

5.5 Purely Spiritual Warriors or Actual Soldiers?

Learning Objectives

In this unit you will:

- examine the role of Sikh soldiers, particularly in the UN
- explain how Sikh beliefs influence their views on resolving conflict
- reflect on your own views about ways of resolving conflicts.

Starter

- What do you know about the wars going on in the world today?

There have been many conflicts throughout human history. However, some of the events of the Second World War were so horrific that an international organization was set up to try to avoid anything like that happening again. It's called the United Nations, or the UN, and it has mainly a peacekeeping role. During conflicts, soldiers provided by UN member states will go out to the affected areas and act as peacemakers and protectors. They are often identified by their light blue helmets and white vehicles.

There are many Sikh soldiers who work as UN peacekeepers. Their role is to defend and protect others in order to keep the peace.

As part of their identity as warriors, Sikhs (following the example of Guru Gobind Singh) often practice martial arts as preparation for any kind of conflict. The mental focus that martial arts require makes it an almost spiritual experience. The Guru started the festival of Hola Maholla, so that Sikhs could practise their military exercises and hold mock battles.

? Are you surprised to see Sikhs involved in the military? Do you think it's natural to see a religious believer involved in conflict? What could they be fighting for or against?

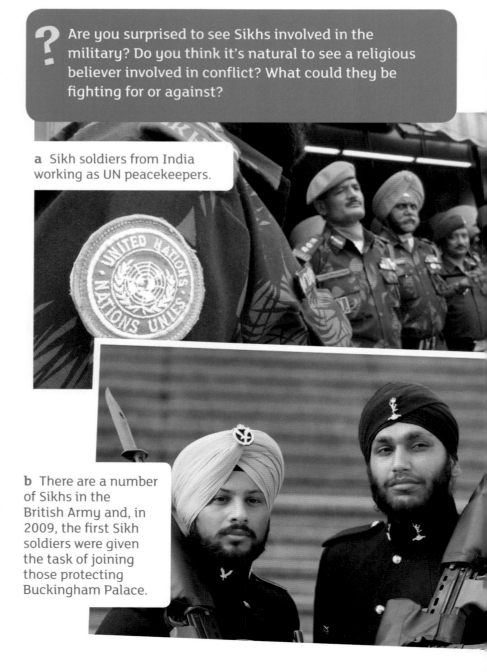

a Sikh soldiers from India working as UN peacekeepers.

b There are a number of Sikhs in the British Army and, in 2009, the first Sikh soldiers were given the task of joining those protecting Buckingham Palace.

Case Study

How do Sikhs respond to conflict?

Sikhs don't have a war just for the sake of having a war. We do it to save people, so they have no worries in their life; we see everyone as brothers and sisters. But if [those brothers and sisters] have done something bad, we will fight against that.

In the summer of 2011, riots erupted across Britain following the death of Mark Duggan, who was shot dead by police in London. It has been said that the rioting was caused by several different factors, including anger over racism, economic decline and gang culture. There was destruction, looting, fighting and unrest across many communities.

Balwir describes the role of Sikhs at that time as defenders. Sikhs, he explains, protected properties and people – staying out of the fighting and looting and supporting those in need.

Balwir's father, Mr Singh, adds that he stayed up all night during the riots – looking out for any trouble and contacting the police when needed. He supported his neighbours and the extended local community, keeping them informed and feeling safe.

c The summer riots of 2011.

Reflection

What would you be prepared to fight for physically? And spiritually?

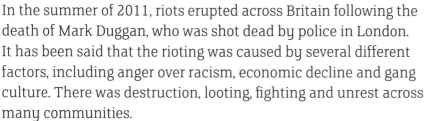

Activities

1. Think about what you have learned about the Gurus. Do you think any of them would support fighting in a war?

2. Do some research to find out more about the United Nations. What is the Declaration of Human Rights? What does it say about war and resolving conflicts?

3. Explain, in your own words, what the role of the UN is. Why do you think Sikhs support it?

4. 'Violence and conflict are never the answer.' Respond to this statement by referring to your own beliefs and those that a Sikh might hold.

5. Write a newspaper report or TV news item about the responses of Sikhs during the 2011 riots. Include an interview with Balwir.

5.6 A Faith Living Amongst Faiths

Learning Objectives

In this unit you will:

- examine how Sikhs understand their faith in the light of other faiths

- analyse Sikh teachings about other faiths

- ask questions about whether any religion can be better or more relevant than another.

Starter

- Do you think that all religions should get on with each other?

- Are faith and religion the same thing?

Sikhism was founded during a time when Hinduism and Islam were the predominant faiths, and there were a number of disputes about the correctness of the way Hindus and Muslims practised their religion. Guru Nanak tried to remove the religious conflicts and taught that the only way was the way of the One True God. The Guru respected the faiths of both Hinduism and Islam and, in fact, one of his close companions was Mardana, a Muslim. Guru Nanak affirmed that all those that believe in One God, irrespective of their religion, are the creation of God. In a hymn in the Guru Granth Sahib the following is sung:

? Some people say that all religions believe in the same God and are simply climbing up different sides of the same mountain. What do you think? Would a Sikh agree with you? Do you think there could ever be one world religion? Why or why not?

> *'The One God is our father; we are [all] the children of the One God.'*
> Raag Sorath, Guru Granth Sahib p.611

a

Many argue that people believe in a religion as something man-made, and that they are losing sight of God at the heart of it all. Many Sikh teachings and practices suggest otherwise. Guru Gobind Singh taught: 'As out of a single fire, millions of sparks arise; So from God's form emerge all creation, animate and inanimate.' (Akal Ustat, p.87)

Sikhs believe that God does not make the judgements that humans make about each other – in His eyes we are not any better or worse than any other human.

Sikhs are involved in interfaith groups all over the world. In Britain Lord Singh of Wimbledon is the Vice Chair of The National Inter Faith Forum which has just celebrated its 25th anniversary. The aim of this group is for people of all faiths to work together for cooperation and understanding.

> **?** How does the quotation from Guru Gobind Singh suggest Sikhs should treat all those around them, including those of other faiths?

b Lord Singh of Wimbledon.

Reflection

'All you need is God, not religion.' What do you think? Present your ideas in groups.

Activities

1. If you look at the two teachings quoted in this unit and remove the fact that they are from Sikhism, would you have known what religion they had come from? Explain your answer, with reference to other faiths.

2. If you agree with the 'mountain' explanation on the left-hand page, transfer this into your book and explain why. If you don't, create an image or diagram that sums up how you see all the world religions. Do they believe in totally different things? Or the same things?

3. What kind of society do you think we would have if everyone believed in the Sikh teachings in this unit?

4. 'People are just too different. There will never be peace between the faiths, so why try?' Look back over what you have learned in this unit and respond to this quote from a Sikh perspective, and then from your perspective – comparing the two.

Sikh Beliefs in Action

Objectives

- Explain how religious teachings guide Sikhs' moral and ethical actions and choices.
- Reflect on and identify where guidance and direction can come from in life.

Task

'My faith: It is all I need.'

Your task is to write a news article for a smartphone news app from the point of view of a Sikh, using the statement above as the headline.

A bit of guidance...

- Your article should be between 200 and 300 words long.
- It should include one image and two quotations
- The quotations can be from the Guru Granth Sahib, or from other research you have completed
- You will need to look back over the work you have completed in this chapter, and include in your article whether religious faith can guide a believer in how to respond to moral and ethical issues in life, as well as issues of belief.

Hints and tips

- Check that you understand what moral and ethical issues are, and choose some examples from the chapter to illustrate your article
- It is important that you try to present a balanced argument for this task. You will need to explain why believers feel that their faith is all they need, and why others feel that something more is needed
- You have a limited word count, so make sure that you select the information for your article very carefully – deciding what is most relevant
- Make sure that the conclusion to your article includes your views in response to the question generated by your title: 'Is religious faith all a person needs to answer or deal with all the many issues that the world has?'

a

Guidance

What level are you aiming at? Have a look at the grid below to see what you need to do to achieve that level. What would you need to do to improve your work?

	I can...
Level 3	• identify the impact of religious belief and teaching on the lives of believers • make links between my beliefs and values and my choices and behaviour.
Level 4	• make links between the beliefs of a religious group and their responses to moral ethical issues • ask questions about the impact of belief on actions and apply them to my own and others' lives.
Level 5	• explain how religious teachings are used to provide answers to important questions about behaviour and morality • ask questions, and suggest answers to important questions about ethical issues and morality.
Level 6	• explain why religious responses to moral and ethical questions may differ within a faith • give my viewpoint about some important ethical and moral questions, giving reasons and examples, and show how following religious teachings might be a challenge in the modern world.

Ready for more?

When you have completed this task, you can also work on your skills for Levels 6 and 7, and perhaps even higher. This is an extension task.

Imagine that your finished article has created a bit of a stir, and that the company you work for has asked you to put together a debate about the topic.

• You need to choose three well-known people who you think would contribute something useful to the discussion (including key figures from the past, if you want).

• Create a script for the discussion, showing the range of possible responses and bringing out the strengths and weaknesses of the various arguments.

Glossary

Abortion Medically removing a baby from the womb during pregnancy

Akal Purakh A Sikh name for God

Altruism Selfless care and concern for others

Amrit Sanskar The initiation ceremony

Anand Sanskar The marriage ceremony

Antam Sanskar The funeral ceremony

Biodiversity The variety of life in a particular place

Castes Groups and/or divisions within society with higher or lower status than each other

Chaur An implement like a fly whisk that is used to pay respect to the Guru Granth Sahib

Cloning Cultivating DNA to make an exact copy of a living creature

Conception The moment that a sperm fertilizes an egg and a woman becomes pregnant

Creeds Statements of belief, usually religious

Daswandh Giving a tenth of one's salary as a charitable donation

Death row The part of a prison housing those sentenced to death

Deterrent To deter or put others off from committing a crime

Dhan Giving to charity or giving time to others

Embryo testing Scientific testing on a foetus at very early stages of development, usually for medical research

Euthanasia Helping someone else to die

Granthi Someone who is fluent in reading the Guru Granth Sahib

Gurbani Teachings of the Guru found in the Guru Granth Sahib and other religious texts

Gurdwara The Sikh place of worship

Gurmukh Putting God at the centre of your life

Guru A spiritual teacher

Guru Granth Sahib The eternal Guru of the Sikhs, which embodies the teachings of the ten Sikh Gurus

Guru Nanak The founder of Sikhism

Harmony Agreement in thought and deed

Inhumane Cruel; lacking compassion

Injustice Violation of the rights of others

IVF In-vitro fertilization; this treatment helps couples to have children by fertilizing the egg outside the womb and then implanting it back into the woman

Janam Naam Sanskar The naming ceremony

Jakara Sikh salutation

Justice Moral righteousness

Kachera One of the Five Ks; a type of Sikh under-shorts

Kangha One of the Five Ks; a wooden comb

Kara One of the Five Ks; an iron bracelet

Karma A combination of a person's actions, with either a positive or negative outcome in the next life

Kesh One of the Five Ks; uncut hair

Khanda An important Sikh symbol containing three swords and a circle with different meanings

Kirpan One of the Five Ks; a sword

Langar Both the food and the hall in which it is served, at a gurdwara

Man Mental service, such as studying

Manmukh Putting human and materialistic desires at the centre of your life

Meditation Extended thought and contemplation

Mela A big fair or gathering

Mool Mantar The opening prayer in the Guru Granth Sahib, containing the essence of Sikhism, and describing the attributes of God

Mukti Union of the soul with God

Nagar Kirtan A parade led by five Sikhs, to represent the Panj Piare (see Unit 2.6)

Nishan Sahib The Sikh flag

Palki The canopy covering the Guru Granth Sahib

Persecution Persistent ill-treatment, usually because of race or religion

Pilgrimage A holy journey to a place of religious significance

Political prisoners People imprisoned for their political beliefs or actions

Reht Maryada The Sikh code of conduct

Reincarnation A cycle of birth and death and rebirth

Religious experience An experience of God; a spiritual experience

Sacred Holy, or a gift from God

Sacred thread A cord worn as a Hindu rite of passage

Sangat A Sikh congregation

Secular Without religious reference; non-religious

Seva (sewa) Selfless service to God's creation

Shabad The Word of God in Gurbani

Simran Meditating on the word of God; for Sikhs, this must also be completed to balance out seva – to remember God in everything

Soul (atma) The spiritual spark that keeps the body alive

Sustainable Able to be maintained

Takht The 'throne' on which the Guru Granth Sahib is placed

Tan Physical service, for example in the langar

Index

OXFORD
UNIVERSITY PRESS

Great Clarendon Street, Oxford OX2 6DP

Oxford University Press is a department of the University of Oxford.
It furthers the University's objective of excellence in research,
scholarship, and education by publishing worldwide in

Oxford   New York

Auckland   Cape Town   Dar es Salaam   Hong Kong   Karachi
Kuala Lumpur   Madrid   Melbourne   Mexico City   Nairobi
New Delhi   Shanghai   Taipei   Toronto

With offices in

Argentina   Austria   Brazil   Chile   Czech Republic   France   Greece
Guatemala   Hungary   Italy   Japan   Poland   Portugal   Singapore
South Korea   Switzerland   Thailand   Turkey   Ukraine   Vietnam

Oxford is a registered trade mark of Oxford University Press
in the UK and in certain other countries

British Library Cataloguing in Publication Data

Data available

ISBN-13: 978-0-19-838901-9

10 9 8 7 6 5 4 3 2 1

Printed by Bell & Bain Ltd, Glasgow

Acknowledgements

The publishers would like to thank the following for permissions to use their
photographs:

Cover: Narinder Singh: **p10t:** Art Directors & TRIP/Alamy; **p10b:** NASA;
p11: Art Directors & TRIP/Alamy; **p18:** Art Directors & TRIP/Alamy; **p22:**
Art Directors & TRIP/Alamy; **p23tl&b:** Art Directors & TRIP/Alamy; **p23tr:**
PhotosIndia.com RM 14/Alamy; **p24:** Art Directors & TRIP/Alamy; **p25l:** Art
Directors & TRIP/Alamy; **p25r:** World Religions Photo Library/Alamy; **p26:**
AFP/Getty Images; **p29:** Tim Page/CORBIS; **p33:** Maurice Savage/Alamy; **p34:**
Getty Images; **p35:** xanirakx/Shutterstock; **p36:** World Religions Photo Library/
Alamy; **p38:** World Religions Photo Library/Alamy; **p39t:** World Religions Photo
Library/Alamy; **p39b:** Sally and Richard Greenhill/Alamy; **p40l:** AFP/Getty
Images; **p40r:** Gauravjeet Singh Chhina/Demotix/Corbis; **p41:** Maurice Savage/
Alamy; **p42l:** Alex Lentati / Evening Standard /Rex Features; **p42tr:** Paul Doyle/
Alamy; **p42br:** Richard Levine/Alamy; **p45r:** Jag Lall Singh/UNITED SIKHS;
p45l: AFP/Getty Images; **p46:** 2010 AFP/Getty Images; **p47:** www.khalsaaid.org;
p51l: Featureflash/Shutterstock.com; **p51m:** Michal Kowalski/Shutterstock;
p51r: Joe Seer/Shutterstock.com; **p52:** Dennis Donohue/Shutterstock; **p52:**
Dennis Donohue/Shutterstock; **p53t:** With kind permission from EcoSikh;
p53b: Leicester Mercury; **p54t:** With kind permission from Mejindarpal Kaur/
UNITED SIKHS; **p54bl:** Igor Zh./Shutterstock; **p54br:** Bruce Rolff/Shutterstock;
p56: David Taylor/Alamy; **p57:** EDELMANN/SCIENCE PHOTO LIBRARY; **p64:**
clockwise from top left: Art Directors & TRIP/Alamy; Tim Graham/Alamy;
KeystoneUSA-ZUMA/Rex Features; AFP/Getty Images; **p65t:** UNITED SIKHS;
p65b: With kind permission from Mejindarpal Kaur/UNITED SIKHS; **p66t:**
MUNISH SHARMA/Reuters/Corbis; **p66b:** AP/AP/Press Association Images;
p67: Bettmann/CORBIS; **p68:** ZUMA Press, Inc./Alamy; **p69:** World Religions
Photo Library/Alamy; **p70:** With kind permission from Mejindarpal Kaur/
UNITED SIKHS; **p72t:** AFP/Getty Images; **p72b:** Jeff Moore/Jeff Moore/Empics
Entertainment; **p73:** Getty Images; **p75:** 2011 AFP/Getty Images; all other
photos by OUP

Illustrations: Gareth Clarke

From the author, Julie Haigh: Many thanks to both the families who have
helped shape this book with their openness and faith. It has been a pleasure to
work with you. Thanks also to Janice Chan, Lois Durrant, Minh Ha Duong and
Janet Dyson for their help and support. The greatest thanks go to my wonderful
family, Dom and Maia, who have been an endless source of inspiration,
encouragement and love. And, of course, even more cups of tea.

OUP wishes to thank the Singh/Kaur family, the Singh family and Mejindarpal
Kaur for agreeing to take part in the case study films and to be photographed
for this title. We would also like to thank Mejindarpal Kaur and her dedicated
team at UNITED SIKHS for reviewing this book.

We are grateful to the following for permission to reprint extracts from
copyright material:

Dr Kulbir S Thind for Guru Granth Sahib texts as published on www.srigranth.
org, copyright © SriGranth.org. All rights reserved.

EcoSikh and Alliance of Religions and Conservation for vision statement from
www.ecosikh.org.

Living Faiths

Sikhism

Julie Haigh

Series Editor: Janet Dyson   **Consultant:** Robert Bowie

OXFORD
UNIVERSITY PRESS